Ludic Pedagogy

Ludic Pedagogy

A Seriously Fun Way to Teach and Learn

Sharon Lauricella and T. Keith Edmunds

ROWMAN & LITTLEFIELD
Lanham • Boulder • New York • London

Published by Rowman & Littlefield
An imprint of The Rowman & Littlefield Publishing Group, Inc.
4501 Forbes Boulevard, Suite 200, Lanham, Maryland 20706
www.rowman.com

86-90 Paul Street, London EC2A 4NE

Copyright © 2023 by Sharon Lauricella and T. Keith Edmunds

All rights reserved. No part of this book may be reproduced in any form or by any electronic or mechanical means, including information storage and retrieval systems, without written permission from the publisher, except by a reviewer who may quote passages in a review.

British Library Cataloguing in Publication Information Available

Library of Congress Cataloging-in-Publication Data

Names: Lauricella, Sharon, author. | Edmunds, T. Keith, author.
Title: Ludic pedagogy : a seriously fun way to teach and learn / Sharon Lauricella and T. Keith Edmunds.
Description: Lanham : Rowman & Littlefield, 2023. | Includes bibliographical references and index. | Summary: "This book presents, in a lighthearted format, an empirically based pedagogical model for higher education that incorporates fun, play, playfulness, and positivity"—Provided by publisher.
Identifiers: LCCN 2022061453 (print) | LCCN 2022061454 (ebook) | ISBN 9781475871654 (cloth) | ISBN 9781475871661 (paperback) | ISBN 9781475871678 (ebook)
Subjects: LCSH: College teaching—Methodology. | Motivation in education. | Play.
Classification: LCC LB2331 .L26 2023 (print) | LCC LB2331 (ebook) | DDC 378.1/25—dc23/eng/20230215
LC record available at https://lccn.loc.gov/2022061453
LC ebook record available at https://lccn.loc.gov/2022061454

Contents

Foreword		vii
Introduction		xi
1	Fun	1
2	Play	21
3	Playfulness	37
4	Positivity	59
5	Fun and Wellness	75
6	Implementation and Impacts	89
Conclusion		101
Appendix		105
Notes		109
References		115
Index		129
Author Bios		133

Foreword

While Sharon and Keith were writing *Ludic Pedagogy*, I was completing a three-year study on the use and value of play in higher education (HE). We only got to correspond after we had both hit the submit button. And yet, in reading their book, I have found our texts share many resonances: The sad snuffing out of creativity and playfulness as pupils progress through formal education systems. The pedagogic significance of play, despite the difficulties of defining it. The variety and inventiveness that playful learning, or, to use their term, ludic pedagogy, encompasses. The need for discernment in designing playful experiences to suit educators, students, subjects, and contexts. The many myths and assumptions about what play and games in education entail. The false binaries between work and leisure, work and play, study and play.

Although it has been slow in coming, recent years have seen a real growth in interest in, and openness to, play in adult learning. While playful post-compulsory education may not be mainstream, inroads are being made into the suspicion with which it can be regarded. In creating their philosophy of ludic pedagogy, Sharon and Keith anchor themselves firmly in the growing field of scholarship and practices of play at college and university.

Despite this new wave of enthusiasm for play in HE, it is not always easy to be a playful academic; there can be numerous challenges. One is the myth that playful scholars and educators want to destroy traditional academia. A couple might, but for the most part this is fiction. Educators who use play are passionate defenders of the best kind of HE; where students thrive, learn, and grow.

Nothing wrong with a gripping lecture, inspiring seminar, the artistry of an excellent essay, and exams for certain things. Everything is wrong with tired, dull practices which demotivate. Everything is wrong with systems which dictate that certain forms of teaching and assessment are the only way to educate. We all know that decisions about how to teach and assess are often made for expedient reasons (coping with too many students or too little resource), not because they are pinnacle examples of pedagogy.

Another myth: if you take liberties with academic conventions, you cease to count as a legitimate scholar. Academic writing must be sacrosanct. The serious tone, the third-person voice, jargon-filled opacity, and endless polysyllables. Come on, we've all done it. It takes a certain bravery (and terror—I speak from experience) to step away from the familiar and write about play playfully, rather than from a safe, serious distance. But it is perfectly possible to do, without losing quality or substance. Sharon and Keith manage this by writing a book in a style imbued with the four elements of their model: play, playfulness, fun, and positivity. Bouncy, energetic, colloquial sentences *can* cohabit with quotes, theories, and principles written in more traditional voices. Education and entertainment do not need to be either/or. You can have both, along with aspiration, achievement, scholarship, depth, connection, community, laughter, insight, and fun.

Ludic Pedagogy is a resolutely upbeat, joyful, and enthusiastic book. However, it also recognizes that the elements of its model are deep, contradictory, and complex concepts. Not all fun will feel like fun during an experience. That may come after the event. Not all play is joyful, energetic, and sociable. Some are quiet and internal. Our feelings about play and fun are subjective and strongly held. So the authors' advice that we need to think carefully about the kinds of play we want to engage in, and what our playfulness, positivity, and fun will look and feel like, is important.

Educator awareness that play is multifaceted, with sun and shadows, is sometimes overlooked by critics of playful scholarship. One I came across recently complained that if educators are evangelical about play, it must mean that they are uncritical. What does this say about the state of HE today? That we only have academic credibility if we are miserable? Such a generalization ignores the fact that playful educators like Sharon and Keith are well-versed in the nuances, ambiguities, and contradictions of play-based and playful learning. What it may also point to is that educators who advocate for play—often camouflaged or peripheral pedagogy in HE—are having to make a far stronger case than those who are working with familiar and accepted approaches.

With this in mind, a word here for Rowman and Littlefield as well. Despite the increase in visibility, and slowly developing critical mass, of literature on playful postcompulsory education, many publishers are still wary of bringing out books on play. Take a bow for supporting a book that is *all about play*, under its fabulous academic-sounding title.

Like Sharon and Keith, I believe in combining informed irreverence, lightness of touch, informality of tone, and solidity of scholarship while speaking directly to the reader. It helps the author/s connect to the wonderful person who has decided to pick up their book. In this case, this is you. Whether you are new to playful pedagogy or a seasoned practitioner, there will be something for you here. Just as the authors refuse to impose (and rightly so) a single way to play, only you know your academic context, educational culture, drivers, influences, enablers, and constraints. This book offers you a packed, lively, and insightful resource to interpret from where you are, whoever you are. You are in for a rollicking read.

Professor Alison James
December 2022

Alison's latest book, *The Value of Play in HE: A Study*, can be freely downloaded from https://engagingimagination.com

Introduction

In 2006, Judson Laipply recorded and uploaded a six-minute video that he called "The Evolution of Dance" to YouTube. The video features a deadpan Laipply, looking like anyone's friendly next-door neighbor, wearing an Orange Crush t-shirt and butt-hugging jeans, seamlessly executing dance crazes—in chronological order—to music including (but not limited to!) The Twist (Chubby Checker), Mony Mony (Billy Idol), and Dirt Off Your Shoulder (Jay-Z). Laipply's video received over 70 million views in less than eight months. He boasts "the first global viral video" and became the world's first YouTube celebrity (Laipply, 2019).

Why was this video so popular? Its accolades are not pocket change—being the inaugural YouTube celebrity by means of a humble video is a Very Big Deal. It's not every day that someone becomes a YouTube sensation, even in this era of TikTok dances and Instagram reels. The cause for the popularity of Laipply's video is clear. He is having fun. He is enjoying the performance. The audience is having fun. Viewers can hear the crowd laughing and cheering. Laipply's enthusiasm is evident as he moves from illustrating one decade to the next. The whole video—from start to finish—is, quite simply, fun.

Laipply's video is historically accurate and required a great deal of research.[1] There are serious elements here—he had to get the chronology, music, and moves just right in order to accurately hit the adage, "it's funny because it's true." So, his video is not all fun and games—there was a great deal of "work" involved in hitting the sweet spot. The same can be true of academic studies. Success in college and university requires work, there are no two ways about it. But when students get it "right," when they have that "aha" moment, when there's a humorous example, or students get to play with concepts, it becomes, quite simply, fun.

But sadly, the experiences of students in HE tend to fall into two broad categories—the fun stuff and academics. The two might enjoy a small overlap in which students have the elusive, mystical unicorn of a course that is both educational and fun, but at the moment, the two categories are by and large separate and distinct. Life at college and university is like living two different existences on the same campus: one life that is characterized by work, struggle, and stress, and the other that is characterized by fun, laughter, social bonding, and making memories.

The fun stuff—parties, events, residential life, and whatever else the kids these days call fun[2]—plays a key role in post-secondary education. These positive experiences are central to both the attraction and retention of students (Madgett & Belanger, 2008). Prospective students choose a university based on many factors: for example, location, academic program, and fees. And the fun stuff is most certainly part of the decision-making equation. What's the party life like? What do the dormitories or residences offer? Are there clubs, organizations, and events that students can join? Are there opportunities to make friends? The fun stuff is very often not only what attracts students to a particular institution, but student life also plays a significant role in keeping students at universities (Bean, 2005). But the fun stuff for students is—for the most part—limited to out-of-class experiences.[3] The fun stuff is the parties, concerts, pub nights, or beer pong. It's residential life, hanging out in common areas, having late-night nachos, and making TikTok videos with friends.

Why not take the radical view that there is no reason why the academic aspect of HE cannot be part of a student's positive experiences at college or university? What if students had fun in class? What if, when students graduate, they also remember their classes in their nostalgia rather than just the parties and greasy breakfasts while enduring five courses per semester? What if classes were not just a means to an end to get to the weekend when the good times happen? This is not to suggest that Psych101 feature a keg in the lecture hall or that the pizza delivery person comes to the back door of the class. Instead, this model suggests the opportunity exists to offer students more play, laughter, and social bonding *in class* so that learning—spending time in class, thinking about course material, and even doing assignments—is a positive experience that affects overall student wellness *outside of class*. Work and fun need not, and perhaps should not, be separate existences.

The opportunity for more fun is relevant to face-to-face, online, or hybrid/blended teaching and learning environments. For example, face-to-face classes can include more interactive activities so that students collaborate or (gasp!) talk to one another or can involve more hands-on activities. In hybrid or online courses, breakout rooms, chat, and even simple online tools such as polls, word clouds, or quizzes that don't count toward a grade can all be used. No matter the environment, more fun—for both faculty and students—ought to be inherent in the syllabus.

This book outlines a new philosophy for post-secondary education: Ludic Pedagogy. From "ludere," Latin for "to play" or "to play games," Ludic Pedagogy is structured around four elements: fun, play, playfulness, and positivity. This pedagogical model was designed to help reintroduce the joy of discovery into learning.[4] All too often, the innate joyful aspect of learning is sacrificed due to the misguided notion that it is at odds with the goal of maintaining academic rigor. Tweed-jacketed professors may cross their arms and huff at the notion of having fun in a traditional lecture hall with fixed seats arranged in such a way as to adore the sage on the stage, but fun in learning and scholarly prowess are not incompatible ideals. Indeed, research suggests that elements of the Ludic Pedagogy philosophy serve to both better engage students and to enhance learning. For example, Fisher et al (2011) explicitly argue that "play and learning are not incompatible. It is not play versus learning but rather play via learning for which we must strive" (p. 353). Similarly, fun adds excitement to the learning process; hooks (1994) argues that such excitement is fundamental to the learning experience.

The Ludic Pedagogy model was inspired by what gets lost in formal education. Almon (2004) notes that fun and play are the earliest forms of education that children experience. It is through these tools that the most fundamental skills are developed—the basic building blocks upon which rest everything else we learn. Remember games like Operation? Jamming electrified tweezers into Cavity Sam[5] is not only fun but also great for developing and testing fine motor skills. And Perfection—the one where players put yellow shapes into a tray—that's classic sorting and recognition, but it was so fun to try to beat the clock! Card games of all sorts (Uno, SkipBo, or classic card games like Rummy or Hearts) are great for strategy development. Playing games is fundamental to early childhood education—and games like cards never get old for adults.[6]

Yet, despite the important roles held by the concepts of fun and play in the most important stages of our educational (and intellectual and otherwise formative) development, the amount of fun and play afforded to learners is slowly stripped away as children progress through their formal education.

This erosion of fun progresses from the early years of learning through play, until students endure the joyless factory (Leather, Harper & Obee, 2020) or banking (Friere & Ramos, 1970) models of education. By the time students enter high school, the fun and play of formal learning—even the unstructured playtime of recess—has been stripped away and replaced with cheerless lectures and standardized testing. In post-secondary education, institutionally endorsed fun and play—in a learning context—are essentially non-existent. Ludic Pedagogy can change that.

The Model: Fun, Play, Playfulness, and Positivity

There are some students who are intrinsically motivated to attend classes by the idea of the learning itself. Educators are always grateful for the handful of encounters with these actual, real-life mystical creatures they experience over their careers. But the bottom line is that most students attend their university classes for *extrinsically* motivated reasons: to get good grades, a diploma, a degree, eventual career opportunities, and so on.[7] Faculty, administrators, parents, and even students might shrug and think, "oh well, at least they are going to class."

But the problem is that extrinsic incentives negatively impact the process of learning and the students' interest in returning to the topic (Condry, 1977). In other words, if students go to class because they *have* to, they won't learn well and probably won't develop enthusiasm or affinity to course concepts. And they are certainly unlikely to be engaged in the class. So, if the desire is to foster lifelong learners, relying on extrinsic motivators to get these students to class is at cross-purposes.

In contrast, Ludic Pedagogy focuses on students' *intrinsic* motivation. This teaching philosophy seeks to tap into students' desire to learn, interest in course or program concepts, and ability to learn in meaningful ways. Ludic Pedagogy is not a fear-based model: it does not focus on performance or "getting it right." It is based on the notion that learning can be rewarding and fun in and of itself. It can also significantly increase the proportion of intrinsically motivated mystical students—the largest populations of whom will be in classes guided by Ludic Pedagogy.

This pedagogical model is based on four elements: fun, play, playfulness, and positivity. Figure 0.1 outlines the Ludic Pedagogy model.

Fun is the primary motivator in the Ludic Pedagogy teaching philosophy. As they are tripping over sleeping roommates on their way to class, students are ideally thinking, "I *want* to go to this class today," or as they leave, say (preferably aloud), *"That* was fun." But how do faculty and students *actually*

LUDIC PEDAGOGY

FUN is an intrinsic motivator, and is supported by:

Figure 0.1   Ludic Pedagogy Model. *Source*: T. Keith Edmunds.

get to fun? Three fundamental elements support the experience of having fun with learning: play, playfulness, and positivity:

- Play is an *activity*—it is what students and instructors do in the classroom and with course concepts (either physically or mentally); it is a behavior or set of behaviors.
- Playfulness is an *attitude*—it is the way instructors "show up" to class, and how students are encouraged to show up as well; it is the participants' disposition and behavioral intention toward the course, the course content, the learning activities, and any other relevant aspect in the learning environment.
- Positivity is an *affect*—it is how students and instructors approach learning so that they can get the most out of the learning experience; it is the emotional component of the model.

The elements of fun, play, playfulness, and positivity—both separately and together—have been shown to improve student learning, retention, and course outcomes.[8] This book provides both the why and how of each of the Ludic Pedagogy elements so that they can be both developed and utilized to enhance teaching and learning in post-secondary education. Stories and anecdotes (and genuinely hilarious endnotes) are included to illustrate the concepts and to demonstrate how they can be put into practice.

What Ludic Pedagogy Isn't

Ludic Pedagogy is not a prescriptive model. This book will not provide a must-follow script of jokes or a list of specific activities to do that can be checked off to make this pedagogical approach work.[9] The way of Ludic Pedagogy requires authenticity: everyone must embody the philosophy in a way that is their own and rings true to who they are. Everyone has a different sense of humor, ways of relating to students, and various academic areas and courses to teach. Therefore, the philosophy presented within this model, and the ways of internalizing and expressing it, will be unique to each instructor, student, institution, and academic discipline. However, the principles are applicable regardless of one's unique situation or background, and scholarly work will be presented, showing that each of these elements plays a key role in improving and enhancing student learning and the educational experience.[10]

The Ludic Pedagogy model does not suggest that faculty take on the additional (and demanding) role of entertainer in addition to that of educator. It does not imply that instructors must become stand-up comics;[11] however, those who want to be more performative,[12] and can do it authentically, are certainly welcome to do so. This model works for those who see themselves as strictly educators and for those who feel that there is a role for entertainment in the classroom. The key is to take on the elements of fun, play, playfulness, and positivity in ways that are one's own. This means that—as with all good teaching philosophies—scholars will need to reflect and approach teaching in ways that are true to themselves.

Ludic Pedagogy is therefore not a strict recipe that must be followed step-by-step for educational success. Rather, it can be considered as a list of "ingredients" from a few broad categories that can be assembled in any way the scholar likes. One can take some activities to play with, a playful attitude in a way that is authentic, and a spirit of positivity in different measures, at different times, or in different proportions. The mixture can change each week, in each class, or in each course so that the "secret sauce" of fun and challenge can be met.

An Invitation

This book will help you to embrace fun, play, playfulness, and positivity so that your classes contribute as much as possible to your students' success. It will help you to be confident that each of these elements helps your students to learn, retain course information, create social connections, and enjoy their time at college/university. If you take on the action, attitude, and affect described and developed by Ludic Pedagogy, your classes will be memorable—for both you and your students. This book will help you not only justify (necessary) but also fully embrace fun, play, playfulness, and positivity. Join the growing numbers of HE instructors embracing this pedagogical model and create your own stories and experiences practicing and playing with Ludic Pedagogy.

CHAPTER 1

Fun

College and university life comes with a variety of traditions, rituals, and legends. For example, at Emory University in Georgia, "Dooley," the resident campus ghost, is reported to have started writing letters to the campus newspaper in 1899 from his station as a skeleton that functioned as a mute observer in a science lab. Today, Dooley lives on via a secret student in a skeleton costume who appears on campus (surrounded by student guards, of course) a few times per year. Dooley's most noted appearance is during the aptly named "Dooley's Week," which is a declared time of parties and revelry. At the University of Maryland-College Park, students offer food to the campus terrapin turtle statue during finals week in hopes of good grades. The same terrapin is touched before athletic events, again for good luck.

According to Bronner (2012), such traditions and legends at academic institutions are part humor and part ritual, because the stories or traditions are representative of student life—particularly student stresses, fears, or needs. Students strive for academic success, and they enjoy the feeling of being part of a community. Campus rituals might offer cultural advice or cautionary tales, but they all have in common a sense of playfulness. This spirited connection is cultivated because students hear or repeat the tales verbally, thus creating a sense of community with both the institution and fellow students. Quiet whispers of "Do you know the story of . . ." or declarations that "We gotta do this for good luck" have the potential to unite students—and such bonding is often served with a healthy dose of humor and fun.

Students have a reputation for having (or, at the very least, wanting to have) a good time. But let's face it, those good times are usually not in the science lab, lecture halls, or library (though we're sure that there are exceptions, some of which might be the stuff of campus lore). If you are reading this book, it is unlikely you need to be converted to the cause of making classes more fun. However, you are also likely aware of—and are probably personally acquainted with—someone who teaches in higher education and believes that fun has precisely no place in the academy. You know, the one who believes that fun is downright incompatible with serious scholarship and that it has no role whatsoever in the hallowed halls. That their knowledge and wisdom is all students need. That fun is, in fact, the antithesis of everything they stand for. Even if you have a fun-friendly dean (or, maybe you *are* a fun-friendly dean!), one might say, "Show me the data!" This chapter will back you up when justifying, believing in, and creating fun in the classroom.

Quashing fun in the name of rigor is anathema to the true purpose of education. It is well-recognized that fun is an important aspect of learning in early childhood, when arguably the most important learning of our lives takes place: fine motor skill development, social exploration, and language acquisition, to name just a few fundamentals.[1] However, for no good reason, the amount of fun explicitly incorporated into formal education is steadily reduced until it is almost completely removed in high school and even more so in college and university classrooms. Post-secondary students often lament that attending classes is the least fun aspect of their education. Fincham (2016) suggests that "this is not the fault of teachers but of an education system where outcomes are marked by an absence of creativity or joy" (p. 78). Similarly, hooks (1994) notes that in the critical discussion by educators writing about pedagogical practices in the K–12 system, there appears to be no interest among either traditional or radical educators in addressing the role of excitement in higher education.

The Ludic Pedagogy model suggests that it *does* remain within the realm of possibility (or even responsibility) for instructors in higher education to reinstitute fun in the classroom, and this book is here to lay the red carpet for fun's grand entrance into the post-secondary academic environment.

What Is Fun?

"Fun" does not have a widely accepted definition in academic literature, despite its common use and the general recognition of its existence. Part of the issue with defining fun is the myriad ways in which the term can be used. McManus and Furnham (2010) identify fun as being simultaneously used as a motivational concept, a trait concept, a range of behaviors, and a type of social situation. Some authors go much further in attempting to define the term, such as Podilchak's (1991) conceptualization of fun as an interactive process by which people create social and emotionally weighted bonds with their peers.

Fun may be considered as a characteristic of things in which people are engaged, such as tasks, behaviors, or activities. But one can easily envision that what is "fun" to one person could be very much "not fun" to another. For example, skydiving may be fun for thrill-seeking individuals. Crowded house parties may be fun for extroverts. However, sitting quietly with a cup of tea and a good book may be the pinnacle of fun for introverts or intellectuals. What people do, how they think about such activities, and how they feel about them all constitute everyone's perception and understanding of what is "fun." It can be seen, therefore, that "fun" has a behavioral dimension, a cognitive dimension, and an affective dimension (McManus & Furnham, 2010).[2] Based on the wide variety of what might be considered fun, perhaps it is easier to state, "You know fun when you see it." Said differently, "You know fun when you experience it."

Despite the significance of fun in the human experience, there is very little "serious" (i.e., scholarly or academic) study on the topic, perhaps due to its amorphous nature that has, to date, largely resisted definition. Given the parameters of scholarly analysis, it is not in the authors' best interest to provide a strict definition of "fun" in this chapter, and they are unlikely to provide a rigid definition in future iterations of this study.[3] To recycle a joke of which they're quite proud, attempting to establish a definition of fun does not meet the authors' idea of fun.

The Ludic Pedagogy model recognizes fun as a motivator, but also as a trait concept (fun classmates or a fun professor), a range of behaviors (a fun classroom activity), and a type of social situation (a fun class). Mostly, however, the model focuses on the motivational aspect of fun, as it has been designed to highlight activities, attitudes, and affect that serve the idea of fun, thereby motivating students. Fun is also the thing that is focused on when looking at other related concepts: we don't ask people if they are enjoying playing or humor; we ask if they are having fun (Georganta & Montgomery, 2016). In other words, fun is based on what students do and how they feel in the classroom, and if managed correctly, these "dos" and "feels" create the fun that keeps students wanting to come back and learn more.

People are often motivated to do things (such as educational activities) because they enjoy them (that is, they find them to be fun). If the lack of parameters around what constitutes fun is unsatisfactory because you are the kind of scholar who needs a definition that you can underline, take a picture of, then post to social media,[4] this is for you: "fun" is a concept that encapsulates both intrinsic motivation and positive affect in a social environment.

Because both intrinsic motivation and positive affect vary from individual to individual, fun is inherently subjective (McManus & Furnham, 2010). When attempting to incorporate Ludic Pedagogy in the classroom, instructors must remain aware of the fact that fun cannot be forced. Mandated fun is usually no fun at all. Imagine a situation in which you are a student and are told, "You are now going to have fun in this class by engaging in [insert despised activity here]." No, thanks. Not only would such a demand be at cross-purposes with Ludic Pedagogy by failing to instill intrinsic motivation, but it may have also damaged any motivators that could have been in place. On the other hand, encouraging fun is not a sure bet. Students in the classroom may or may not be motivated by a "fun activity."

Keith once tried to motivate students by using candy as a reward for answering questions in class—fun, right? Not for all students. Some students didn't like candy and others were almost insulted that they were being bribed to participate in class. The same issue occurred in a different course with pizza. There were students with dietary restrictions such as gluten-free, lactose-free, or vegan. How can a single motivator possibly serve them all at once?

The tendency for instructors, administrators, and society in general to see a class of students as a homogenous group with the same likes and dislikes is a dangerous temptation. "Kids these days," is the kind of thinking that can lead us into the thinking that "everyone loves pizza."[5] The reality is that students are individuals and what each of them considers good or fun is equally likely to be individual. The differences in perceptions of what *is* and what *is not* fun are based on a range of characteristics, including but not limited to: "demographic differences, hierarchy, role requirements and diversity among people" (Plester et al, 2015, p. 380). And the last thing an instructor wants to do is to alienate a student or group of students in their attempts to have fun!

But all is not lost. Instead of trying to mandate fun, instructors can create conditions that are likely to be conducive to fun. Playful learning and fun can function as intrinsic motivators (Whitton & Langan, 2019). The creation of classroom tools, materials, and activities that hold the *potential* to be fun is the goal of implementing Ludic Pedagogy. As an additional consideration when trying to create fun conditions, ponder this: "If fun is a requirement in education or other activities, then some answer is required as to whose type of fun it should be" (McManus & Furnham, 2010, p. 165).

Much of Ludic Pedagogy is rooted in this management of conditions. As practitioners, we till the metaphorical soil and plant the beans and water the sprouts with the hope and intent that the beanstalk will grow. But therein also lies one of the secrets of this pedagogical model: As we invest time and efforts into creating conditions that we hope will be fun, we are providing ourselves with an environment in which we will experience the same state of fun. In other words, an instructor can have fun *while preparing* to have fun in class. Modeling the experience of fun may in and of itself provide the fertilizer that helps the beanstalk grow. Use this as your own check: if class prep is fun, class probably will be, too. Imagine laughing out loud just thinking about what might happen when students respond to a question or participate in an activity. If you're laughing just imagining it, it's probably going to end up even better.

Ludic Context and Ludic Content

Fun can be present in course *context*, otherwise known as the learning environment. Think: is the "vibe" of the class fun, lighthearted, and engaging? How do students feel as they take a seat, consult the course LMS, or enter the synchronous course meeting? Fun can also be present in course *content*, which refers to course material and learning activities. Think: are the concepts illustrated by means of fun discussions, movement, or experiments? Are students actively involved at times, rather than almost entirely passive (i.e., participating rather than just taking notes)? But better yet, fun can be present in both context *and* content. Fun in the classroom may be understood along two primary streams—fun activities (content) and fun delivery (context) (Tews et al, 2015). Let's take a closer look at both ludic context and ludic content.

Sharon manages classroom context and encourages fun by starting each class meeting with a poll, survey, or word cloud. As students enter the classroom or appear in a Zoom room, she displays an introductory question of the day which usually features a funny image or meme. The "mood scale meme" is particularly effective; this question features nine different photos of one subject, such as cats, dogs, Shrek, Shakespeare, or Kermit the Frog. Students are invited to anonymously choose the image that most suits their state of being on that day via free online polling software, and results are tallied. Sharon then invites students to explain why they identify with, for example, a cat looking exhausted, a dog looking surprised, or Shrek looking smug. This is a helpful "hook" to begin the class period and works particularly well with online classes. This kind of lighthearted activity lets the instructor understand where class members are in terms of their moods on that day. Such activities create friendly, low-stakes dialogue, and therefore create prosocial bonds (Podilchak, 1991). These prosocial bonds are known to be essential in fostering a sense of belonging and cohesion among students, so activities like this serve overall satisfaction with the university experience.

> Dr. Aaron Langille of Cambrian College in Sudbury taught remote, synchronous game design courses throughout the pandemic. Given the option, students chose to be "camera-off" during lectures and activities. One day, in a class that discusses identity expressions in video games, students were tasked with creating an avatar using only free-to-use software or apps—no other instructions. Many students recreated their real-life selves in cartoon likenesses, while others created funny, weird, or fantastical expressions. Having never met in person, these avatars—realistic or otherwise—created a personal connection beyond the black boxes of Zoom. Many students kept the avatars for the remainder of the term, and in courses that would follow. Dr. Langille has repeated this exercise in hybrid (flex) courses, where students attend both in-person and online.

Keith embeds fun into course content via role-play activities to facilitate students' understanding of theory and practice. In the Business Negotiations course, his students practice negotiation skills through a simulated purchase and sale of an intergalactic spaceship. This participatory activity allows for deeper learning of course concepts, such as the difference between positions and interests. The activity also builds specific skills, such as how to address cultural ambiguity. However, the content is discussed and delivered in a way that is just silly enough to make it fun. Certainly, the same concepts could be employed using a more mundane situation such as purchasing a used car, but the surprising content of the simulation gets students' attention and keeps them involved.

The difference between ludic context and content can be further illustrated via fictional[6] comments from students:

Case A: "The prof is great—funny and everything—but the course material they teach is just *so boring*!" [non-ludic content]
Case B: "I'd really enjoy the class—the material is so fascinating—but the prof who teaches it is just *so boring*!" [non-ludic context]

In Example A, the context is fun and playful, but the content does not appear to invite student engagement. The professor seems to have done a good job of integrating a playful attitude into the learning environment. However, the course content still comes off as dry and unengaging. Example B illustrates the opposite. In this case, the student is intrinsically motivated to learn the material, viewing the content itself as fun, but the non-ludic teaching style of the instructor negatively impacts the student's motivation.

In both cases, introducing ludic elements could help to retain the student's interest and engagement. Tews et al (2015) showed that "fun delivery was demonstrated to have a positive relationship with engagement. Fun delivery exhibited the strongest effect with emotional engagement, followed by cognitive engagement and physical engagement" (p. 24). Therefore, ludic context sets a favorable stage for learning. Furthermore, play can elevate interest and engagement. When students find academic material interesting—such as when they are enrolled in courses within their major—allowing students to learn by interacting with it through play can only serve to increase the amount of learning taking place. Playfulness could also serve to emphasize and enhance a student's interest in learning. The ideas of play and playfulness are further explored in later chapters.[7]

Fun and Cognitive Load

Fun motivates students, but the benefits of "academic fun" extend well beyond motivation. One of the most important benefits of fun is associated with cognitive load, or the amount of working memory that is used when learning or thinking. For example, cognitive load is raised in the presence of distractions, such as cell phones and social media (Frein, Jones, & Gerrow, 2013), because students place memory and thought in a variety of places. Students in impoverished conditions also experience increased cognitive load (Mani, Mullainathan, Shafir, & Zhao, 2013) given the challenges outside of learning and memory—such as hunger and safety—that they must address. By contrast, fun lightens the cognitive load and helps make learning easier. When an academic task is conducted in a fun or lighthearted context, the amount of memory and "thinking" involved is significantly lower. This reduced cognitive load, according to Van Winkle (2017), results in increased levels of learning. In other words, fun in the classroom not only motivates students to learn, but also makes it easier for them to do so.[8]

The relationship between fun and learning can be considered in the context of Cognitive Load Theory (CLT) (Sweller, 1988), which outlines how cognitive resources are utilized during problem-solving and learning processes. According to CLT, there are three parts to a learner's cognitive load: (1) *germane cognitive load*, which deals with the cognitive activities that promote learning; (2) *intrinsic cognitive load*, the part that is imposed by the learning task itself, and (3) *extraneous cognitive load*, or the additional cognitive load resulting from the method by which the new material is presented (Hu et al, 2017).

According to CLT, when we teach new material, the content should not be presented in such a way as to create a high level of unnecessary cognitive load (extraneous cognitive load) (Chandler & Sweller, 1991). When we integrate fun into the learning activities through play or playfulness, for example, we reduce the overall cognitive load by moving that which would normally be extraneous cognitive load into the intrinsic cognitive load. By making learning fun and thereby tapping into the intrinsic load, the overall cognitive load is reduced. All of this theoretical brain function talk ultimately means that not only does fun better motivate students to learn, but it also improves their ability to learn. To boil down, distill, and caramelize these studies on cognitive load: Learning is easier when it is fun.

It might be easy to get defensive and say, "Well, sure. For some courses it might be easy to make learning fun. But it can't be done in *my* course." That's a hard "nope." There are very few, if any, courses that cannot incorporate some fun (even if it is unexpected laughter, weird examples, or surprising comparisons). In a rather corporeal example, Hu et al (2017) explained how fun activities and assignments regarding animal (and human) urination are used to teach principles in both biology and engineering. Because it would be irresponsible (and probably infuriating) for us to leave it there without explanation—here's what they did: The authors know that most people would question the legitimacy of a study showing that most animals urinate, on average, for about 21 seconds.[9] But wait, how do scientists even collect that information? Students presented with this query will be particularly curious about how this study was conducted and how the results were tabulated. Such curiosity allows the instructors to introduce more sophisticated ideas in order to explain the 21-second urination phenomenon. Engineering instructors can introduce the function of a variety of hydraulic models and how they function. Biology instructors can address evolutionary excretory functions or can have students research various animals' bladder sizes and urethra lengths. Hu's team used this fun introduction to a more serious academic concept through the example of the cheekily named "Golden Rule" to engage students.

If You Can't Make It Fun, Don't Make It Not Fun

Given that fun is subjective—that is, what's fun or not fun varies from person to person—it might feel that the means by which we can create fun is actually quite elusive. If we picture a lecture hall with immovable seats, a podium at the front, and mobile whiteboards,[10] it may even feel downright impossible. We acknowledge the inexorable fact that no one can mandate fun. Try to force it and it will end in tears. In these cases, rather than trying to make such situations fun when the fun simply won't take, all hope is not lost. We can take small steps toward fun by just trying to make things not un-fun, or delete the double negative, and just try to make things not boring. In other words, we can focus on not killing the conditions that might allow for fun to blossom and holding space for fun to spontaneously erupt. Nature abhors a vacuum, after all, so if we leave space for fun, chances are, fun will take the invitation.

The name of the game with Ludic Pedagogy is to create the opportunity to have fun, and then to cultivate and sustain it as best we can. Along these lines, Podilchak's (1985) conditions that inhibit fun can be considered and recast in the positive to present five conditions that can cultivate fun or, at the very least, contribute to the potential success of a fun environment.

1. Instructors must engage in the fun activity.

    If an instructor functions as a bystander or passive supervisor rather than an active member in an online or classroom activity, the sense of fun is quashed, quelled, and quit. Perhaps the instructor is lacking a sense of playfulness or feels a bit self-conscious. We're all human. Yet we know that modeling on the part of the instructor is very powerful. Students are far more likely to engage in an activity that the instructor themselves dives into without reservation. In other words, you need to be willing to jump in and have fun (or, in some cases, actually *start* the fun) if you are going to expect it from your students. Don't ask them to do anything you are not willing to do yourself!

    For example, in a course on Nonviolent Communication (NVC), Sharon introduces an activity in which students are asked to fold a paper crane. She explains that in order to leave class that day, students must have a crane in order to get out the door (even if it is ugly, half-baked, or even folded by someone else). For some students—and, admittedly, the instructor—folding a crane is simply not in their spatial capacity. So, Sharon sits at an empty desk alongside students, and struggles with an increasingly mangled piece of origami paper. Some students do the same, while others whip up their cranes in a matter of moments (often with the help of YouTube, online instructions, or one another). It is possible that some students might be tempted to just quit and slide out the door, but knowing that the instructor is struggling with the same challenge that they are provides students with a sense of community. There is no shortage of laughs in this fun activity, for there are some very unsightly "cranes" produced.

2. Address emotional and physical safety concerns.

Amy Poehler said, "No one looks stupid when they're having fun." But sometimes having fun means being willing to at least *feel* silly, if not look silly. Being willing to look silly, unreserved, or unsure among peers, particularly among young adults in post-secondary settings, requires a sense of psychological safety. As the facilitator of fun activities, we must be sure that all settings are safe in every way.

Without a sense of safety, attempts at encouraging fun could backfire. Research shows that if students feel that their participation is *required* in an activity, fun or not, they may engage in such an activity even if it makes them feel uncomfortable or embarrassed (Plester, Cooper-Thomas, & Winquist, 2015). These negative feelings may result in disengaging the student from the class, the student skipping class, and/or increasing levels of stress and other negative effects. All of these outcomes are directly counter to the intentions of Ludic Pedagogy. Therefore, any attempt to encourage fun in the classroom must consider safety: physical, psychological, and emotional.

For example, in an introductory course in Public Speaking, Sharon runs an activity on barriers to listening. The activity is held either outside on the grass or in a large, empty classroom. It begins with students pairing up, then choosing one to wear a blindfold, while the other becomes a guide. Sharon then scatters plastic Easter eggs with a variety of treats inside them (inspirational messages, candy, erasers, etc.) over a wide area. On her cue, the guide verbally leads the sightless partner around to pick up as many eggs as possible. The activity can get loud, and there is a lot of laughter. Some students feel self-conscious and participate cautiously, and still, others don't even bother to listen to their guide and rampantly throw caution to the wind in order to try to collect as many eggs as possible. Safety is a significant issue in this activity: physically, students must not collide with each other or objects, and emotionally, students need to feel comfortable enough to participate. Such safety is a barrier to listening, which is discussed in the activity debrief. In order to be mindful of emotional safety, this activity is conducted toward the end of the semester, when students in the course are more likely to feel comfortable with one another and have an increased sense of trust in the instructor. Once the activity is introduced, students preferring to be a "referee" or supporter are invited to do so. Overall, students enjoy this silly but illustrative activity, and the debrief is lively.

3. Equity, diversity, and inclusion must be top of mind.

When designing fun activities, be sure to give careful consideration to any potential inequities. Any activities that exclude a participant based on ability, sex, age, or race will introduce inequities and thus immediately negate any opportunity for fun. Similarly, asking students to bring expensive equipment is unacceptable, unless it is in the course outline as a requirement, such as in engineering or sciences. Besides thinking carefully about any potential inequities, it is a good idea to have a colleague or trusted fellow educator review any activities that you're not sure about. This check-in could be with someone you know, or with the strong and helpful community on #AcademicTwitter; social media can be a great way to float ideas, get new ones, seek and give advice, or think out loud.

4. Be mindful of stress levels/fatigue/overwhelm.

The rite of passage of attending university seems to include falling asleep somewhere—in class, the library, a bench, under a tree, anywhere, really. And students have lives outside the classroom. Many are employed either on or off campus, and it is likely that students are under a deluge of midterms all in the same week. While we often cannot do much to ease these kinds of situations, we can remain aware of them and help guide students to existing supports, if appropriate. In other words, we cannot always take low levels of engagement or non-engagement as a commentary on our fun-ness.

Sharon conducts an activity in her third-year ethics class in which students experiment with "The Trolley Problem." This activity measures tension in students' declared ethical framework and the choices that they make in specific situations. Previous iterations of this activity have always been fun and lively. One particular year, it was a total flop. Students just didn't seem to enjoy it. Rather than force the activity along, or convince herself that she is a terrible instructor, Sharon asked, "Is something wrong? Everyone just seems so off." Students explained that they had a midterm earlier that day in another class and that most of the students in this cohort had barely slept the previous night. Sometimes, if students aren't buying in, it's not about you. Just ask.

5. Make sure the props/supplies work.

Be warned: tech is notorious for failing at just the wrong time. We all know firsthand that absent-minded professors forget things at home, in their offices, or in their cars. Things break. Dogs eat homework. Students are normally very forgiving when something doesn't go according to plan.

But as Abraham Lincoln (purportedly) said, "If you give me six hours to chop down a tree, I will spend the first three sharpening the axe." In other words, be prepared. If you get students engaged in a fun learning activity, you have them primed and motivated to learn. Negatively impacting this opportunity due to a breakdown in a prop/tool/supply would be heartbreaking. You heard it here: have Plans B, C, D, and maybe E.[11]

There is a well-known story that continues to circulate in one of the authors' institutions about an instructor who, many years ago, was excitedly explaining rules of grammar to a perhaps somewhat less-enthusiastic group of students.[12] Emphatically explaining when the prepositions "on" and "in" were and were not interchangeable, the instructor took a big step onto their[13] desk to illustrate "on." Perhaps they thought they were channeling Robin Williams' character in *Good Will Hunting*. Maybe they were carried away. Maybe they were just trying to make a dry topic more fun. In any case, as the instructor took a broad step from the floor to stand on their desk, an audible *riiiiiiiip* echoed through the room, leaving the instructor stranded on the desk and the entire back end of their pants, uh, we'll just let you imagine the rest. Though this incident happened over a decade ago, at least one of this instructor's colleagues still keeps an extra pair of pants in the office. Just in case.

Class can be fun. Class can be real. Class can be real fun. But fun cannot *guarantee* that learning will occur. What is most important, though, is that fun is an incredibly powerful motivational tool. That motivation itself might be all that is required for some students to cross the threshold from resistance to learning (Francis, 2013).

The Social Element(s) of Fun

Many people—introverts, in particular—can get a great deal of pleasure and enjoyment from solitary activities. Lots of academics enjoy knitting, a good Netflix binge, or a puzzle/crossword/word search/brain teaser. But fun, by its very nature, is largely a social phenomenon. Although pleasure and fun are terms that are frequently used interchangeably, Fine and Corte (2017) assert that pleasure and fun "have an important sociological distinction. Pleasure is personal, an experience of individual actors, while fun is social" (p. 67). In other words, pleasure is something that someone usually takes part in without someone else's participation, but fun involves other people.

Any classroom configuration, properly organized, can be considered a social environment by most reasonable definitions.[14] At a minimum, there is some sort of social interaction between the individual student and the instructor. A study of adult learners found that their concept of fun included the contributions of the teachers, in addition to learning processes, approaches, and strategies (Lucardie, 2014). Being involved with a student by providing some degree of personalized instruction can be evaluated by the student as adding to the fun. Certainly, this makes sense, as attending a dry lecture on a difficult topic while being an anonymous face in a sea of anonymous faces is far from anyone's idea of fun.

Interaction between students is arguably the most relevant aspect of the social elements of fun in class. As previously lamented, too often the social element of fun in higher education exists only outside the classroom environment—save for the shuffling in and out of class, and perhaps the backchannel discussions or chat. However, classrooms are comprised of groups of students that can be reasonably assumed to socialize outside the classroom. It therefore takes only a little bit of imagination to transmute that sociability to the classroom. Certainly, this sociability needs to be managed and focused on specific learning goals but introducing fun by means of social interaction is really just this simple: allow it to arise organically between students.

> In my fourth year of university, we took an off-campus trip in an elective, experiential learning course. Part of that trip was the inevitable socializing, which brought people closer together. I remember looking around and seeing everyone laughing, smiling, dancing, and telling stories. It was just a beautiful memory. There was one classmate who was very quiet and reserved. He came to an outdoor gathering where one of our class members played DJ and everyone was dancing. Suddenly, our quiet classmate got up and did the most uninhibited dancing that I have ever seen. It was literally "dance like no one is watching" kind of dancing. He was amazing! It really made me think about how being yourself can bring such joy to others. Our in-class experiences were different after that because our inhibitions were down. Ironically, we had our reserved classmate to thank for that. The fun vibe that we had on our trip transferred into class time afterward, which was really valuable.
> —R. Budd, Student, Bachelor's, Ontario Tech

The metaphor of tending and tilling a field can help illustrate the cultivation of sociability and fun in class. Instructors plant the seeds of fun and cultivate the conditions for it to grow—but then have faith that the seeds will be fruitful. Likewise, when fun is encouraged and cultivated in the classroom, communication and sense of community is more likely to develop. Research suggests that in fun environments, "individuals may be less concerned with protecting their images and be more open to exploration and making mistakes" (Tews et al, 2017, p. 47). That is, students can become less self-conscious and willing to step out of their self-constructed social barriers in order to connect with others or to participate in activities. Even further, fun encourages the development and maintenance of positive emotions. In simpler terms, having fun makes people feel good. A positive emotional environment can be conducive to creating new or improved relationships, and such an environment can also mitigate some of the anxiety associated with learning new things while simultaneously encouraging the willingness to do so.

As a very simple example, students in Sharon's fourth-year NVC course take on a rather open-ended semester-long project. Some students immediately know the details of what they want to accomplish via this project—it is often something they've always wanted to do in their studies but haven't had the opportunity to take on yet. However, other students can become mentally paralyzed by choice—this is often the first time that they've been given so much academic freedom. In order to give students the time and space to work through ideas and ask questions with their peers before submitting a project proposal, Sharon invites social interaction, which turns out to be quite fun. She prepares a bag full of squares of different patterned paper (purchased from a craft shop). Students are asked to randomly choose a piece of paper from the bag. Then students are to identify other people with the same pattern on their paper, find a place to meet, and discuss their plans or challenges with their project ideas.

This very simple activity is helpful because it gets students moving around and gives them the opportunity to talk in a safe and boundaried environment with people they haven't previously met. As a bonus, the activity also reduces questions asked of the instructor because students help one another to brainstorm and clarify potential issues. While sometimes students groan at the idea of having to move seats and extricate themselves from the security of their laptops or tablets, the unanimous sentiment at the conclusion of the activity is, "Well, that was fun and helpful!"

Clearly, fun among students is not just fun for fun's sake.

Shared fun deepens relationships: When social interaction is effective, people feel good. Relationships can flourish. This doesn't mean that every course or class meeting time is going to be hearts and flowers and rainbows and unicorns, with everyone holding hands in raptured unity. But there are ways of being mindful that the fun encouraged in our classrooms and labs is inclusive of student diversity. Community and celebration of diversity is to be encouraged rather than boundaries between in-groups and out-groups. The key to this element of successful fun is in how the students perceive the activity or environment presented to them.

Theory suggests that individuals evaluate situations (activities, environments, circumstances, etc.) against their personal mental construct of fun before deciding whether or not they will engage in or with it. If the situation aligns with the—in this case—student's idea of fun, they will decide that it will be fun and will engage. However, if there is a significant difference between the situation and the student's construct of fun, they will likely decide against engaging (Middleton et al, 1992).[15] It therefore becomes the responsibility of the instructor to adequately frame the situation such that it matches with students' constructs of fun. Obviously, this can only be done if the instructor understands their students, which in turn means that it becomes difficult to have a template of fun that can be reapplied or repurposed class after class, semester after semester. Each group of students will be different and will understand the fun in different terms. For example, when referring to examples in popular culture, we must be mindful to choose figures or events that are contemporary and relevant to the age cohort with whom we are interacting.[16]

Part of whether a higher education student perceives an activity as being fun or not is relative to whether or not they perceive *meaningfulness* in it (Middleton et al, 1992). In other words, is the present activity relevant to the course? Is it applicable to the specific topic on that day? When introducing an activity, it is best practice to go beyond simply explaining what an activity is (or will be), and to clearly illustrate the *value* of the activity. With value comes meaningfulness, and with an understanding of the meaningfulness comes a greater likelihood of students evaluating the activity as fun.

For example, students in Sharon's NVC class participate in an activity that results in a timeline of nonviolent events. Each student is given a laminated card of an historical event relative to nonviolent conflict resolution. Students engage with one another to arrange themselves in chronological order according to the card that they hold. When introducing this activity, Sharon explains: "This activity gives us an appreciation of the history of nonviolence. You'll learn about new events and see other events that you knew about with a new perspective." An explanation of the value of the activity gives students context and helps them to understand *why* they can participate in this activity.

Zinn (2008) explains the complexity and opportunity of fun in learning: "Fun in learning . . . cannot be defined by a single word and is primarily about the satisfaction that comes from serious immersion in meaningful educational and intellectual experiences that empower students as successful learners and connect school to their hopes and dreams for their lives" (p. 154). Through social interaction and developing an understanding of meaningfulness, once again, it is clear that fun enhances learning.

> I took a deep breath and stepped out of my office dressed as the Greek goddess Athena. My historically inaccurate Amazon purchase had me in a "Roman Spartan Costume Helmet," a "Roman Empress" costume over my clothes, holding a large plastic spear and a "Wonder Woman" shield. It was the best I could piece together online, and it would have to do—and this was for fun!
>
> In our Reacting to the Past (RTTP) game, The Threshold of Democracy: Athens in 403 B.C., the students had to self-start their first Athenian Assembly debate by reenacting a pig sacrifice (pig picture torn in half) while priestesses of Athena offered prayers. The president sat at his table, ready to start the proceedings. They were nervous. I was nervous for them.
>
> So, in a flourish of polyester and plastic I stomped into the classroom. I banged my spear on my Wonder Woman shield and stood behind the shocked priestesses. I whispered, "Go for it!"
>
> Student faces were a mix of shock and amusement; I was certainly not cool enough for a couple of them. But who cared? My priestesses pulled it off, the pig was sacrificed, and the president called the meeting to order. They debated and voted. The next week I gave extra credit for showing up in a toga, and about 20 percent of the class came wrapped in random bedsheets. In preparation for our five-session role-playing game, I told them repeatedly to "just have fun with it!" and fun was had!
>
> At the end of the game, I had students fill out a "Win Sheet" where they discussed what they accomplished and reflected on their own gameplay. Paraphrases of some responses ranged from "I didn't think that this would be fun, but it was," and "I have never liked history before," to "I normally don't speak up in class, but this helped me overcome that" and "I met new people and made friends." I took that for a win.
>
> —Melissa Ortiz Berry, Faculty, Bushnell University

Fun Doesn't Mean Easy

The most significant (but blatantly false) argument against fun is fun equals easy. Too many scholars believe that if a course or an activity in class is fun to do, there must be a significant lack of rigor and valid scholarship. In other words, such hardliners believe that fun dilutes or waters down the value of higher education.

Pump the brakes. Hold the phone. Chill out. Fun and scholarship are not binary opposites. They are not even that far apart on whatever arbitrary scale is used to measure such things.

Papert (1996), in writing about technology in schools, coined the term "hard fun." Hard fun is the concept that an activity can be fun because it is challenging, and because it pushes the individual to think or reflect more than they would under other less fun circumstances. Consider the silly, quick games you play on your phone[17]—if a game is too easy, you'll quickly become bored and stop playing. This situation is directly analogous to the classroom: students are simply not engaged with material or activities that are too simple or basic. Sometimes, students disengage not because academic material is too difficult—they wander off (mentally or even physically) because it is too easy.

The "hardness" of learning can refer to three different kinds of difficulty: the hardness of the concept being learned; the hardness of the learning associated with the concept, and the hardness of the attitudinal change associated with the learning (Barret, 2005). The difficulty in each of these does not reduce the opportunities to make learning fun. Video game designers know very well that difficulty—a challenge—is crucial to player engagement. These challenges provide learners with the opportunity to gain mastery over the concept. Challenges, which perhaps initially seem almost insurmountable at the outset, define the learning goals and provide a goalpost against which learners can measure their progress. And when the student can then solve the problem or understand the process or experience the change in attitude, the emotional reward of pride or mastery (or even relief) awaits them (Bateman, 2009).

Making classes fun by making them easy, then, is directly counter to the primary aim of Ludic Pedagogy: engaging students. Hard fun means that learning is fun not because it is easy, but because it is hard. The cool part is that hard learning is still fun, as characterized by the laughter, enjoyment, creativity, and all of those things that it brings about. Hard fun is perhaps best described, somewhat poetically, by Barrett (2005): "Fun without hardness is frivolity. Hardness without fun is drudgery" (p. 122).

Here's an illustration of "hard fun": Rich Little teaches a Microeconomics course that is offered in Assiniboine Community College's Business program. One year, a regular class meeting fell on Halloween. Rich is always looking for new and interesting and, ideally, fun ways to engage students, so he took the opportunity to apply his course content in a novel way. Dressed as Angus Young, lead guitarist of the hard rock band AC/DC,[18] Rich began the class by playing the video for AC/DC's song "Dirty Deeds, Done Dirt Cheap." Following the students' laughter and a brief discussion of favorite music genres,[19] he introduced a data set that showed the supply and demand prices for a "dirty deed" in a fictional, perfectly competitive market. The students applied previous learning from the course to identify the mechanical equilibrium, after which they worked through other economic implications regarding price, perceived value (are dirty deeds really dirt cheap?), and solutions for non-price markets, among others. Rich remained in costume, if not character, throughout the entirety of the class.

Rich's AC/DC example demonstrates "hard fun" because new and potentially difficult concepts in economics are not being made easier for the students. Instead, the same problematic concepts are being presented in a fun manner—both in terms of content and context—such that the students enjoy themselves more, cognitive load is lightened, comprehension is increased, and retention of information is more likely. One would be hard-pressed to suggest that this particular economics class lacked rigor because the instructor introduced fun.

To really inject some caffeine into this argument, one could say that taking the fun out of higher education (or, simply maintaining its un-fun-ness) can negatively impact student engagement, and even make it more difficult for students to learn. This possibility, despite its dramatic overture, is very real: in the context of learning, fun is a psychological need. Glasser (1998) suggests that fun is a biological reward for learning, and humans are hard-wired for both learning and fun. In other words, people have an innate desire to learn, and it feels fun when we finally "get it." In evolutionary terms, we are direct descendants of those who gained an advantage from their learning. Future research could address how *not* having fun negatively impacts learning environments. But it may have a tough time passing Research Ethics Board approval.[20] Nevertheless, making classrooms fun may not take us to the next stage of human evolution in the short term, but it is sure to engage students and assist them in learning academic material more effectively and to a greater degree.

Conclusion

Fun is not a value-add. It's not an "extra" or a "bonus," and it shouldn't be the anomaly in university courses. Fun is in the best interest of students, and it ought to be inherent in every course and class meeting.[21] Seeing as no one ever really recovers psychologically from the "starved student" days of grad school, a couple of food analogies may be appreciated. As discussed, Ludic Pedagogy can be like a stew, with a variety of ingredients all simmered together. Or, a course can be like a great cake whereby the elements of fun, play, playfulness, and positivity are all "baked in." Regardless, each instructor's recipe is different, but the ingredients remain the same. The benefits of the combination of fun and learning are simply too great to overlook.

Research across a range of situations and disciplines shows that creating, allowing, or otherwise simply having fun in class leads to higher engagement in the course, higher engagement with the course material, and higher engagement between and among students (Purinton & Burke, 2019). If we are sincerely interested in helping our students to succeed, fun needs to be part of the equation.

Fun can make learning in higher education less scary, significantly easier, and more memorable. Fun in the classroom can communicate to students that taking social or emotional risks and making mistakes is not only acceptable but is often an essential part of the learning process. Furthermore, the increased social connections resulting from fun improve students' sense of psychological safety and security. This increased sense of safety, which can also be considered confidence, encourages more robust participation from all students; this is particularly true for those who may have been more hesitant to engage with other students or with the course in general. Finally, because fun may energize students, they may have increased "resources to devote to the learning process" (Tews et al, 2015, p. 21). The arguments for fun are clear, and the examples in this chapter illustrate how some of us are doing this already. In order to help you cultivate your own recipe for Ludic Pedagogy, subsequent chapters will address how to leverage play, playfulness, and positivity—all in the name of fun.

CHAPTER 2

∼

Play

> Imagine a place of learning where progressive failing, building resilience and developing individual and collective skills, values, and creativity are not only thought about as a theoretical exercise, but fostered within the pedagogic culture. A place where academic drive is created and nurtured through joy, engagement and play, where learning to solve problems and overcome obstacles is a reward in its own right. Is this not what learning is about? (Koeners & Francis, 2020, p. 143)

Imagine, indeed! Most of us can't even remember a classroom like this, because we were too young when we were there.

Play, whether unstructured or through the use of games, is very often children's first experience of learning (Francis, 2012). And while play is well-entrenched in the early years of education, the idea of combining play and learning seems to end (or is at least significantly diminished) by the end of elementary school. Expecting play in high school or secondary education is laughable.[1]

But the vaporizing of play as education progresses doesn't happen because we age out of the desire to play. Adults typically play less than children, but they only engage in play "when they have the time and inclination" (Bateson, 2014, p. 102). For adults, play must often be scheduled, such as with a group playing recreational hockey,[2] Ultimate Frisbee league, family game nights, or even playing in a band. Sometimes play happens naturally when messing about with a hobby such as woodworking or cooking. But the bottom line is, play just doesn't happen enough once we get "serious," or when we "grow up."[3]

Ludic Pedagogy invites both play and learning, regardless of one's academic level, perceived seriousness, or knowledge of any subject.

Too often, "serious academics" will scoff at the idea that play and learning can coexist in higher education. They assume that play has no place in the academy. That higher education is a serious business. That formal education in universities and college is work. "Rigor!" they shout. "Academic rigor!"

What a bunch of stodgy, old killjoys.

Play is an inherently rewarding activity. What's more, people are more likely to engage in activities that allow for play (Bateson, 2014). This means that motivation is increased when play is involved—and this remains true for any activity, whether it is in the service of learning, work, or leisure. So, it follows that some form of play in the classroom is likely to better engage students.

Much of the concern about play in the classroom is not necessarily about students' learning itself, but about assessment and performance. While a discussion of grades, evaluations, assignments, and assessments could be a book of its own, it is vitally important to consider the words of Koeners and Francis (2020): "our obsession with performance perpetuates an environment with less interest in learning, reduced desire for attempting challenges and a decline in creativity, resulting in poorer standards of learning and work" (p. 150). In other words, measuring performance sucks the fun out of play. Once the element of being watched, evaluated, and supervised is added, play just loses its allure. A hyper-focus on performance is arguably why many young athletes stop their sports when they become too competitive. Such an emphasis on performance, regardless of context, has the potential to outweigh safety, happiness, fun, and enjoyment.

But play and learning aren't always comfortable bedfellows. Starbuck and Webster (1991) suggest that learning might be one of the most complex—but beneficial—consequences of play. This complexity occurs because most play encourages learners to spend time and energy on specific activities. That is, when play-like activities are aligned with course content, play and learning become the same thing. And that thing becomes engaging and pleasurable. Fun.

So, really, come on! "Play has no place in the academy"?!? Research suggests otherwise—and the citations are so plentiful that there is no way we can cite them all in this book. The amount of material that we cut from this chapter alone could fill a book.[4]

What Is Play?

Now convinced that play is the way, you probably want to understand how to embed play into your classrooms. So, what the heck *is* play? How do you know when you have created an activity that meets the standards of play?

Eberle (2014) provides two distinct definitions:

(1) "Play is an ancient, voluntary, 'emergent' process driven by pleasure that yet strengthens our muscles, instructs our social skills, tempers and deepens our positive emotions, and enables a state of balance that leaves us poised to play some more" (p. 231), and

(2) "at its most maddeningly imprecise, play becomes an evaluative and emotive term such as 'art' or 'love,' carrying social, moral, and aesthetic freight that adds to the challenge of defining the word and the concept" (p. 217).

There are probably more definitions of play than there are recipes for apple pie.[5] Definitions and recipes come with a great deal of frantic armwaving and/or frustratingly restrictive results, but despite all of this competition to be right, play-oriented scholars have their hearts in the right place. Spiriosu (1989) frees us from trying to pin Jell-O to the wall: "Play is one of those elusive phenomena that can never be contained within a systematic scholarly treatise" (p. xi). Of course, this doesn't stop scholars from trying. And it doesn't stop apple pie contests, either.

The inability to either precisely or concisely define play (or other foundational concepts of Ludic Pedagogy for that matter) is part of the flexibility and allure of the LP model. The ambiguity baked into these entwined underpinnings gives iron to the strength of Ludic Pedagogy. Consider that all learning is a form of problem-solving. Solving problems in an ambiguous context is one of the primary skills instructors—particularly within higher education—seek to impart to their students. The inability (or downright unwillingness) to precisely define and pin down what is or is not play other than at an instinctual, emotive level means that the pedagogical groundwork being laid is ambiguous. All learning that occurs in a ludic framework strengthens students' abilities to operate in an uncertain environment. Of course, uncertainty and ambiguity can be part of the definition of play itself. Play can be considered a method by which we exercise our feelings and train our minds (Brown, 2010), both of which are necessary for dealing with ambiguity.

> In my Integrated Design Five course, students work in teams of four or five for the entire semester, undertaking both research and design work. This requires teamwork and leadership to be part of the course pedagogy, including negotiation and conflict resolution. As an early semester activity, I pit the student teams against one another in a game of "Survivor

ID5." The teams must work together to decipher a series of clues dispersed on our small campus, with two teams eliminated at each stage. To be successful, the team members must get to know each other's strengths (who solves riddles well, who runs fast, etc.), and choose a strategy: stay together to consolidate brain power, or split up to cover more of the campus footprint? The final two teams must solve a puzzle (just like on the TV show), with one earning bragging rights (and some college swag).

I've used games pedagogically in this class before (including a game show format to teach students how to navigate a zoning ordinance), and a little friendly competition gets the students engaged in the material and fosters an interest in participation. Survivor ID5 introduces the need to know what skills your teammates bring to an assignment, which is important when working collaboratively on complex design projects. Any early-semester lethargy gets worked out, as the pace of the game requires them to sprint around campus. In addition to being entertaining to watch, this activity provides a break from conventional classroom learning, which is too often passive and sedentary.

—Edward Orlowski, Faculty, Bachelor's, Lawrence Technological University

Ludic Pedagogy is not interested in putting play into a prescribed box. Rather, the LP model wants to take play out of the box and allow instructors to do with it what they will to help their students learn. Fussing over a definition of play and placing it into categories and divisions or assigning new names and terminologies does nothing to assist us in understanding or, perhaps more importantly, using play. We know play when we see play. Play is apple-cheeked and full-bodied—it is not dissected and categorized.

Critics are sure to tut-tut the suggestion that play is exempt from a definition. For that reason alone,[6] an operational definition of "play" is provided so that you can use it in a faculty meeting of your choosing. Aligning nicely with the Ludic Pedagogy model, Van Vleet and Feeney (2015) define play as "an activity that is carried out for the purpose of amusement and fun, that is approached with an enthusiastic and in-the-moment attitude, and that is highly-interactive" (p. 632). In other words, play is an activity intrinsically motivated by fun, pleasure, and enjoyment. Shouldn't learning be fun?

Sutton-Smith (1997) and Eberle (2014) identify elements of play that clearly lend themselves to acting as pedagogical tools: humor, skill, pretense, fantasy, risk, contest, celebrations, exploration and discovery, speculation, deception, role reversal, playful startling, socializing, learning, collecting and assembling, synchronizing, cooperating, synthesizing, balancing, and tracking. Many educators will immediately recognize some of these elements of play that they use and/or have used in their practice. Chances are, you've already got an idea of not only what play is, but you've also done at least one activity that fits the bill.

Recognizing Play

When watching someone or a group of people engaged in play, there are activities, behaviors, or actions that tell us, "That's it!" These could be laughter, interaction among participants, or even body language. Eberle (2014) got all academic about play and identified five basic qualities of play: it is (1) apparently purposeless; (2) voluntary; (3) outside the ordinary; (4) fun; and (5) focused on rules. If these qualities are considered as criteria, particularly in association with the reluctantly-stated-but-probably-necessary definition of play above, they can be recognized and applied in the design of classroom activities.

Sharon takes her students camping as part of an elective course in Listening. One of the first things that the group does is make sure that everyone knows one another's names. Tired of the "introduce a partner" activities or alliteration clues (you know, "Ketchup Keith" or "Silly Sharon"), the group gets moving and talking right away by standing in a large circle, all facing inward. On the word "GO!" all participants rush into the center of the circle, where each person finds another and introduces themselves: "Hi, I'm Sandra. Hi, I'm Mario." The two switch identities: Sandra becomes Mario, while Mario becomes Sandra. Then, Sandra (the real, original one) introduces herself to another person in that confused mass of people by saying, "Hi, I'm Mario." Likewise, Mario introduces himself by saying, "Hi, I'm Sandra." The process continues, students trading identities at every introduction. Once someone gets their own, true name back, they return to the perimeter of the circle and remain silent. In the end, when there are only two people remaining within the reformed circle, they should have one another's names, but it doesn't always work out that way!

We can analyze this activity in keeping with Eberle's (2014) criteria for play:

1. *Play exists for its own sake.* The learning attached to play must be emergent. Telling students to "play this game, it's good for you" reduces the play-ness of play, turning it into something else (i.e., something not fun or even boring, aka "an assignment"). Allowing students to

play with the constructs of the course allows their learning to arise on its own. Certainly, instructors may choose to construct the conditions around play in order to guide the emergence of desired learning outcomes. Alternately, the explicit nature of the intended learning can be explored in a debriefing period after the time of play is done.

In the case of the communicative name game described above, the activity is funny, a little raucous, and evokes laughter. The activity is seemingly pointless in that names are exchanged repeatedly. In the debrief, students expressed that they had to listen carefully to the name that they heard, because after the first round, the names that they learned were not the names associated with the face that they saw. Students also had to listen carefully to the directions of the game. Debriefing was key, and students could also ask, "Ok, so who's actually Mario, because I know it's not me!" See? Emergent learning.

2. *Players must choose to play.* In most cases in higher education, we are dealing with individuals who have voluntarily chosen to advance their learning. If we present a strong case for the value of learning, odds are that learners will voluntarily immerse themselves into the learning activities set before them. Play, as one of these activities, will most likely be accepted. Again, however, those students hesitant to participate in an activity that may, at least initially, seem frivolous or silly should be assured of and perhaps guided through the educational value. While such an explicit discussion of play may seem to negate Point 1, the reality is that if the play activity is well-structured, players are likely to begin to play for the sake of play—the underlying purpose is temporarily forgotten.

The name game, as described above, is low-stakes, and no one is likely to be embarrassed because everyone is in the same situation. Given the non-punitive nature of the game, the choice to participate becomes easier.

3. *Play is special.* If we had Christmas every day, it wouldn't be special. Play, to a degree, is the same. Play is set apart from daily activities and exists in its own time and space. In other words, there needs to be a clear demarcation between when play begins and when it ends. When playing in the classroom, perhaps it is as simple as getting students out of their seats, creating virtual groups, or making an announcement that an activity will begin and end.

The time of play is special and should be clearly identified. When students participate in the name game, they know when the game begins, and they knew when it ends. The start and finish of the debriefing is also clearly marked. The "out of the ordinary" aspect of the name game is established by the start and finish of the game and the overall chaotic movement within the activity.

4. *Play is fun.* Honestly, the two go together like Forrest and Jenny.[7] Can play be called play if it isn't fun? If it isn't fun, it's work. And if it isn't fun and it isn't work, we don't do it.[8]

    The fact that play is fun is what makes it intrinsically motivating. We want to engage in play for the rewarding sensation of fun. However, as stated by Eberle (2014), play being fun "is not so simple as it sounds because people can find fun in a dizzying variety of activities" (p. 215). Fun is not fun to everyone, and this can create a challenge: when fun is subjective, whether or not play is worth engaging in also becomes subjective.

    Using the name game as an example again, most students find it fun. However, hearing-impaired students or those with mobility issues might not find it fun at all. It is therefore important to carefully consider the needs of individuals, characteristics of the group, and the environment (i.e., size of the room, weather, etc.).

5. *Play follows rules.* Even Calvin and Hobbes's Calvinball has rules. Rules exist not only to ensure fairness or to provide structure for the players, but also to keep players interested. They are the tenets that keep play moving. Sometimes the rules to play are argumentatively negotiated, as in Calvinball, or they can be highly prescriptive and resistant to alternative interpretations as in the case of most professional sports. Rules don't define play; they are part of play.

    The rules in the name game are part of what makes it interesting and funny. The absurdity of switching names makes the game both more difficult and more hilarious. But the rules in this game are what makes it work and what gives a clear end to the game. The rules also infer whether everyone actually followed the rules at the end, for if the two final players' names are not matched, then someone messed up somewhere (which also adds to the humor).

These five criteria can serve as a checklist when designing a classroom activity that seeks to incorporate play. Is the activity self-sufficient in that it can happen on its own and can be interpreted after its completion? Can students opt-in? Have you created circumstances whereby students want to opt-in? Is the activity different or out of the ordinary? Is the behavior that students exhibit different from when they're not engaged in play during class? Is the activity fun? Can the activity be adjusted or interpreted in order for all students to enjoy it? Are there parameters, guidelines, objectives, and boundaries so that students understand how to conduct themselves and interact with others?

All of these criteria are good guidelines for doing any activity—never mind if it is supposed to count as play or not. All these checkpoints are broad enough to be applied in any academic discipline, any level from first year to fourth, or in any size course. Our job as faculty is to find the kind and style of play that work for us, our students, our courses, and our institutions. This is no small task, but not necessarily unenjoyable, especially if it is made into a game.

Other models of play exist—Bateson's (2014) model of play, for example. These additional models allow an even wider net to be cast by thinking a bit more broadly about what play might look like in classroom activities and how to introduce it into teaching practice. In this case, Bateson's (2014) features of play are similar to Eberle's, but

1. Play behaviors are intrinsically rewarding to the individual—in other words, play is fun.
2. Play may appear to have "no immediate practical goal or benefit" (p. 100). Play is not a behavior similar to work or other serious tasks because it may exist solely for the sake of fun.
3. Because play encourages new ways of thinking and acting, play can lead to the development of new, novel, creative ideas and activities.
4. Play behaviors appear different from non-play behaviors.
5. Because play only tends to occur in situations where stressors do not prevent such behavior in the individual, it may be considered a signal of well-being.
6. Generally, playful play occurs hand-in-hand with positive affect, leading individuals to be more likely to think and behave in more flexible and spontaneous ways.

These models provide us with other ways of thinking about play and how it can support learning in the classroom. Take any study or model of play you choose—find the one that you prefer—and you are likely to gain some additional insight into how it can benefit learning.

Play Is More than Gamification

Play is an inside job. It must be supported by an internal desire to engage—play just can't be forced. For example, no child will continue playing youth soccer unless they want to, and adults won't do crafts or beer league hockey unless they are feeling it. A classic source on play argues that, of "all patterned human activities, play is supposed to depend least on external incentives" (Csikszentmihalyi, 1975).

Play comes from within. Because play can be incorporated into learning, so too can learning and intrinsic motivation[9] be paired. One of the most obvious ways to do this is via games. Gamification has received much attention in academic circles, but play does not equal gamification. There's a real difference: gamification of academic activities risks replacing one form of extrinsic motivator (grades) with another (points/badges/etc.) (Koeners & Francis, 2020). When there are tangible rewards, points, or "winning," play no longer exists for its own sake.

Learning activities can be gamified, so long as the focus remains on the fun of the game rather than extrinsic motivators such as points, winning, or bragging rights. When extrinsic rewards become paramount, they erode intrinsic motivation to play the game in the first place (Deci et al, 1999). The context then shifts from a cooperative community of learning to a competitive environment. Such competition may act as a detriment to learning for many students —not everyone plays to win.[10]

An emphasis on extrinsic motivators and competition has led many instructors to ditch *gamifying learning* in favor of *game-based learning*. While definitions of both gamification and game-based learning vary widely (Plass, Homer & Kinzer, 2015), the primary difference between the two concepts is how an incentive system is used (if at all). Gamified learning involves extrinsic rewards such as ranking, accumulation of points, and competition. It implements game elements—stars, points, leaderboards, and the like—into learning, but does not introduce a fully formed game. In game-based learning, the main focus is on the game—and therefore the play—itself. It's like *Whose Line Is It Anyway*—"everything is made up and the points don't matter."

Game-based learning may be considered a subset of "serious games." While it sounds like an oxymoron—or at least a misnomer—a serious game is a fully developed game that is used to deliver learning objectives (Al Fatta et al, 2019). That is, when instructional and pedagogical elements are incorporated into a game, it becomes a "serious game" (Zyda, 2005).

Games, by their nature, are designed to be fun, and the addition of pedagogy should not subtract from the fun. Scholars of serious games suggest that the pedagogical element in any serious game should not dominate the experience. Rather, pedagogy should be secondary or subordinate to the game, and entertainment should come first. Once entertainment has been worked out, the pedagogy will follow (Zyda, 2005, p. 26).

Laamarti et al (2014) provide a number of examples of serious games, including one used to help train surgical residents on procedures for knee replacements. A video game, much like standard first-person "shooters," provided students a view of an operating room from the point of view of an orthopedic surgeon. Highlighting objects or other individuals in the room allows the player/student to interact with these selectable items. At each step in the procedure, the player is asked questions to test their knowledge. Upon completing the entire surgical procedure, players are provided feedback on the questions they did not answer correctly, the tools they selected out of order, and their overall score. To increase the realism of the game, background sounds are recordings made of actual knee replacement procedures (Cowan et al, 2010). This may not be a game that the general public will be aching to run out and purchase, but in terms of a serious game where learning is a primary concern—awesome!

Play and Ludic Pedagogy

There is some circular logic to the Ludic Pedagogy model: if one can implement play within an environment of learning, and if that play is learning itself, learning has successfully been made an enjoyable, self-fulfilling goal. Learning itself is play, and as play exists for its own sake, a lifelong learner has been created.

A noble goal if ever there was one for an educator.

Play, however, is not enough: it requires playfulness and positivity. And "requires" is not an overstatement. Koeners and Francis (2020) explain that due to brain physiology and chemistry, when individuals engage in play, and do so with the absence of positive emotions, the result can be aggression and anxiety.[11] Both of these outcomes are undesirable, particularly in learning contexts.

Positive affect when coupled with play helps to create a sense of community in the classroom. By playing with their classmates, students engage in genuine human interaction, which creates a sense of safety in that environment. In turn, this heightened sense of safety can help reduce some emotional barriers to learning (Forbes, 2021).

Consider motivation: if we can explain and present the desirability of play—that is, make clear that we are asking the students to have fun—they will be more willing to engage with the activities presented to them. They will not have to be forced, cajoled, or exposed to other techniques of negative connotation to encourage participation. Not only does the opportunity for play and related fun motivate students to engage in the learning activity, but it also motivates them to continue with it. We can rely on the intrinsic motivator of fun without the extrinsic motivators of grades (Walsh, 2015), ranking, or judgment.

Using Play in the Classroom

Forbes (2021) studied play in learning in a higher education context and identified clear themes in incorporating play in post-secondary learning: play cultivated relational safety and a warm classroom environment, it removed barriers to learning, it awakened students' positive affect and emotion, and play ignited an open and engaged learning stance to enhance learning. Clearly, there are myriad benefits of using play in conjunction with learning. However, Forbes also identified an irony: play is under-utilized and even devalued in higher education (p. 62).

It is therefore up to us to champion play in our learning environments—classrooms and all. We can do this by not struggling with designing play to support learning outcomes, but by designing activities in which play may become an emergent property. So instead of struggling with the question of "how do I incorporate play into my classes?" we can look to some basic principles (Eberle, 2014) to help us build activities that are more likely to lend themselves to play.

1. Play originates in anticipation and an act of imagination.

    Students need to have a basic understanding of course concepts. Ludic Pedagogy helps students to anticipate more advanced ideas in the course once this foundation has been established. Once students understand these principles, they can begin to manipulate and play with ideas and concepts. But play begins with anticipation: as students begin to see the form of new concepts emerging from the mists, and as tension and excitement begin to build, the act of imagination begins: *What can I do with this idea?*

2. Surprise.

    Discovery is a dividend of play (Eberle, 2014). In other words, simply by playing, learning very often occurs. The common childhood activity of coloring, for example, teaches manual dexterity. Perhaps the most common application of this idea is through discovery learning approaches when students, through the guidance of an instructor, figure out the intended lessons or material (Hammer, 1997). By embedding it into an environment in which these outcomes can be discovered through play, the student's learning is more impactful and the learning environment is more flexible. Both of these features move the teaching situation away from the rigid standards that promote student disengagement (Pale, 2013).

Cornillie et al (2011) provide an example of how an adventure role-playing game can aid in the learning of a second language. Through a player's interaction with non-player characters (NPCs) in the game, unfamiliar vocabulary may be introduced. Allowing the player to request clarification about the meaning of a word allows the NPC to provide a clarification, thus stimulating vocabulary acquisition in a manner very similar to natural language learning methods (as in through one-to-one conversation).

3. The pleasure derived from play encourages even more play.

   Play and fun are closely associated with pleasure. When people like doing something or derive pleasure from doing it, they want more. Therefore, play is self-rewarding and self-perpetuating. The reciprocal and self-fulfilling relationship of play and fun is a key underpinning of Ludic Pedagogy: learning can be fun, and it ought to be so![12]

   From their feedback, Keith knows that students in his Negotiations class enjoy the weekly role-play activities. Because they are structured to be fun and student engagement in the activities is what is deemed as important, students look forward to these learning opportunities each week. The students acknowledge the valuable learning that takes place, but also indicate the enjoyability of the learning activities—regardless of whether or not they "win" the weekly negotiation.

4. Play leads to understanding, which, in turn, increases empathy and insight.

   Play can help students to understand academic concepts. Once students understand theories, ideas, arguments, or formulas, they can then focus on insight, problem-solving, or design. The development of students' empathy is normally not an explicit learning objective; however, its development as a by-product of play can only serve to improve peer-to-peer relationships in the classroom and enhance the overall learning environment.

5. Understanding, through play, leads to stronger minds and bodies.

   "Play trains our physical skills, sharpens our mental abilities, and deepens our insights into our social capabilities" (Eberle, 2014, p. 225). The feats of strength that arise through play prepare students not only for Festivus,[13] but for real-world challenges. Whether the challenges faced by students are physical, mental, or social, the development of skills through play helps students to face them down and triumph. Oftentimes, the skills gained by students through play are by-products of the desired learning outcomes, so the nay-sayer may question the value of examining this particular element of play. However, although we may introduce play to assist students with the aim to enhance learning on a particular concept, the ultimate goal of any teacher should be the improvement of the students' life. How can life not be improved if teaching methods "accidentally" serve to strengthen the minds and bodies of students? Let's say students are collecting data in a forest, field, or lake: physical exercise is an added bonus, not a detriment.

6. Successful play develops greater poise in the player.
   Beyond the physical and cognitive benefits of play, many authors have noted the emotional and social gains that can be acquired—dignity, ease, contentment, fulfillment, spontaneity, and balance (Eberle, 2014; Zhang & Kaufman, 2015; Zheng et al, 2020, as examples). Regardless of the specific course content presented through play, these bonus outcomes are hard to see as negative, as they can only help in students' development. Role-play, for example, helps to develop peer-to-peer communication, reduce social anxiety, and builds self-confidence (not to mention that students can become friends).

Challenges with Play in the Classroom

Despite the many benefits of implementing play in the classroom, it is not without its difficulties. Leather, Harper and Obee (2020), identified several issues facing play in higher education:

1. Often, the learning that takes place in the classroom is subject to the political pressures of the institution, in that "student outcomes are measured and teaching performance assessed" (p. 209). The Western educational system is based on measurement, ranking, and performance. How can valuable developmental benefits such as an increase in curiosity, the ability to share time and space, or validating others be quantified?
2. Sometimes, faculty believe that effectively implementing play in the classroom requires a great deal of time, skill, organization, and perhaps other resources. While this may be true for larger or more complex play activities, introducing play elements need not be time- or resource-intensive. Many online games are easy to learn, manage, and use in class (see Lauricella & Edmunds, 2022b for suggestions).

3. Because play moves control of the classroom in part into the hands of the players—students—some instructors may feel threatened by the possibility of lack of control, potential disruption of lesson plans, technology failures, or worry about risks. These concerns may be the reason for "cultural mistrust of play in educational contexts" (Leather et al, 2020, p. 209). Overcoming this mistrust requires instructors to adopt a more playful attitude toward their classroom, activities, and students.[14] To quote Gloria Steinem (2019), "making a damn fool of yourself is absolutely essential."

> My most memorable experience was the listening class trip that we took to Ganaraska Forest. We participated in many fun activities during the trip, but the one that was most memorable to me was the night walk. I learned so much that night about myself, and about nature. This is what happened during the activity: We went on a hike at night with our guide. He did not use any flashlights. He advised that our eyes would adjust after so many minutes, and they did. We were walking in the forest in pitch black. That part alone amazed me! We then stopped as a group. Our guide told us we were going to walk a portion of the trail alone, without using any lights, and he would be waiting at the end of the path. He explained that we had to walk straight for about 200 meters and then there was a turn. A lot of us were scared to do this activity, but we had to trust each other. Our guide made me the group anchor who would stay behind and go last to make sure everyone was spaced out and walking the path alone. I got to talk to every person in my class before they did this nerve-wracking activity.
>
> We all bonded so much in this moment. We all learned to trust each other. In the end, we were all impressed with ourselves that we made it through without any issues. I'll never forget this activity!
>
> —Vanessa D., Student, Bachelor's, Ontario Tech

All of these issues are important, and all can be overcome. Assess your own teaching content and context: consider what subjects must be covered, which ones lend themselves best to play, and whether activities will be online, face-to-face, or blended. Consider your own self-awareness regarding how comfortable you are with your students, the course content, and with technology or props associated with each play activity. With these considerations, anyone can begin to implement play in the classroom. Experimentation is key: by keeping the explicit learning outcomes of the course in mind, instructors can develop play activities that support clear objectives. Through successive iterations and conversations with both students and colleagues, play can become a fully integrated element in anyone's teaching practice. You're not likely to get it perfect the first time but keep trying!

With play clearly and explicitly connected to institutionally sanctioned learning outcomes, and with a wealth of research supporting play as a valid and valuable learning tool, many nay-saying administrators are likely to back down. If you find yourself in a situation where this is not the case, solve the issue by rebranding your activity from "play" to "active learning."[15] Active learning seems not to have the same PR issues as play.

Conclusion

Higher education is changing in a multitude of ways, but not necessarily in the right ways. Debates are raging regarding undergraduate courses being increasingly delivered online and programs becoming more industry-focused. Discussions about practical skills and traditional theoretical knowledge are present in faculty meetings at all different academic levels and in a variety of disciplines. Dialogues about traditional versus non-traditional grading schemes are occurring in teaching and learning centers. With these shifts in mind, discussion around course delivery ought to extend well beyond superficial discussions and more toward pedagogy itself.

Students are more likely to stay in their chosen institution, program, and courses if they have positive experiences therein (Madgett & Belanger, 2008). Students are also more likely to succeed if they make friends and feel included in the academic environment. Deciding whether to deliver courses online or face-to-face (or a combination of the two) is not the fundamental question facing academia. Rather, consider whether students have the opportunity to explore, examine, and literally mess around with course concepts. In other words, is there play? Can students do this messing about on their own while online? In small groups either online or face-to-face? In a large class, no matter the delivery method? The opportunity for play is where we as instructors ought to be focusing our energies rather than considering the superficial query of face-to-face or online.

Play is one of the utmost forms of learning. Kolb and Kolb (2010) suggest that play requires students to take the initiative in their own learning, is focused on experience (rather than grades), and invites repeated engagement with the same material, thus improving learning. The simple fact is that play is enjoyable in itself. Regardless of its other benefits, play is fun (Csikszentmihalyi, 1975).

CHAPTER 3

Playfulness

In 2012, Dwyer and Davidson set out to substantiate the claim that people fear public speaking more than they fear death. Turns out it's true. Public speaking is selected more often as a common fear than any other fear—including death![1] It is really no surprise—stories of bursting out in tears, saying the wrong word (i.e., "marijuana" instead of "marinara" during school announcements), passing out, and even wetting one's pants are the stuff of either urban legend or legitimate personal embarrassment (Dobrogosz, 2021). Sharon teaches a first-year Public Speaking course, and there is requisite anxiety, drama, angst, and fear among students (even the ones who take it as an elective because they want to face their fears!).

To start the first class, Sharon asks students to take three minutes to draw a picture of why they are taking this course (it could be on paper if the class is in person, or if it is in online format, students can illustrate via the draw function in Word, on Canva, Google Drawings, or any design program that students like). After a few minutes, students are assigned a partner to discuss their drawing. After requisite laughs at "how bad" their drawing is, students discuss their reasons for joining the course. Then two pairs join into groups of four, and then two groups of four form a group of eight. After groups of eight meet to discuss their "why" of Public Speaking, the class meets as a whole to address who is in class and why they are there.

This playful exercise helps students to meet one another, get comfortable doing something silly with a drawing, and it is their first attempt at audience analysis—a key element in a successful speech. The playful element of a bad drawing (not for grades, obviously!) puts students at ease and introduces laughter into the very first class meeting.

What Is Playfulness?

In the classroom inspired by Ludic Pedagogy, fun is the intrinsic motivator that engages students. Play is the activity element of the ludic educational life—play is the act of doing things. The next pillar in the model is playfulness, the attitude component.

In adults, playfulness is an inclination toward creativity, curiosity, sense of humor, pleasure, and spontaneity (Guitard, Ferland, & Dutil, 2005). Such an orientation to the world, for adults, provides a sort of freedom, allowing us to engage in activities with a willingness to see new possibilities, not restricted by any particular boundaries—real or imagined. When in a playful state of mind, difficulties are but obstacles to overcome, much like in a video game where players meet challenges as problem-solving opportunities or instances to use or increase their skill.[2] In these situations, failures are not failures at all, but opportunities to identify what does not work. Through these low-stakes experiences, players can learn, develop, and grow.

When playfulness in adults is defined as having an attitude toward fun, the value of such an attribute to both professor and student can be identified. Instructor playfulness creates an environment more conducive to learning. The environment is more pleasant and—let's be honest—more fun. Playful instructors demonstrate enthusiasm for their subject matter, perhaps presenting with humorous anecdotes to illustrate important points. Students, approaching classroom activities with a similar sense of playfulness, are less likely to be discouraged and will have improved learning outcomes because they do not experience serious deterrents or punitive consequences from challenges, errors, or setbacks. Like in a video game, students can learn what does not work and can try again with the aim of a better outcome.[3] However, systems need to be in place that not only allow, but encourage, such a playful orientation.

While Guitard, Ferland and Dutil's (2005) definition of playfulness is a good start, it is far from the first or final word in terms of defining the concept of playfulness. Academic literature in education addresses the notion of playfulness, but owing to a wide range of ways in which playfulness is studied and methods by which it is measured, studies of playfulness often do not provide a clear definition of what playfulness actually is (Hung et al, 2016). You may have some sort of vague idea of what playfulness is, too, but as this is a Very Academic Book, we'll try to help you better formulate the concept with the help of relevant literature.

Often, playfulness is represented as a trait (Shen et al, 2014, for example). The Playfulness Scale for Adults[4] identified five important factors in this predisposition to play: being fun-loving, a sense of humor, silliness, informality, and whimsy (Schaefer & Greenberg, 1997). However, Proyer et al (2021) found that interventions such as asking individuals to use their playfulness differently from what they usually do (such as being playful in the workplace instead of only during leisure time) can lead to increased playfulness in individuals. Therefore, if the trait of playfulness can be cultivated, then it must be considered a proximal trait (a trait individuals are able to change and develop over time). While some personalities[5] are more predisposed to playfulness than others, playfulness is not best described or defined as a trait.

Instead, the Ludic Pedagogy model conceptualizes playfulness as an attitude. Playfulness is a way of showing up, looking at situations, and considering solutions. The definition of playfulness in this model more closely resembles Pichlmair's (2008) idea that

> Playfulness is an [. . .] attitude, a mental state of openness towards a situation. [. . .] Playfulness can manifest in any act allowing for limited freedom. If the structures were not limiting, playfulness could not occur. Playfulness is an attitude manifesting in the experience of approaching these limits, of exploring them. (p. 250)

The specifics of these limits will depend entirely on the course content, instructor, students, institution, and a whole raft of other stuff. The point being that too many limits will not allow for any freedom, while an absolute lack of limits is simply chaos. Limits are not meant to be suffocating, but to provide the structure needed for education to take place, even if those limits are simply adhering to the course learning objectives.

> In undergrad, we had a course that had a lot of matrix algebra. Every class had matrices full of 0, 1 and -1. As you can imagine, that can be kind of dry, but at the same time, you need to pay attention. A classmate made up a bunch of bingo cards full of matrices and sold them to the class for a dime. The prof writing his first matrix on the board was surprised by a shout of "Bingo!" We all still remember this 40+ years later—even the long-retired prof, last time I talked to him at a reunion. We were "the class that played bingo in Systems."
>
> The ingenuity and silliness of viewing matrices as bingo, making the cards and selling them and people playing along competitively (such as it was) was part of the memory, but the prof playing along with the silliness

was a big part. I think knowing the prof had a sense of humor gave us all freedom to play.

It wasn't a planned, educational game, and if you tried to make it a game, it would be contrived and ineffective. The bingo/game aspect would be irrelevant and off-topic from the lecture / lesson. The prof had to stay on topic, but the students were able to do it because we had the space to hold two realities in our heads at once. We could engage with the matrices as math, but also as bingo.

What enabled having space was the cultivation of meta awareness and sense making on our own. Now as a prof, the "rules" discourage us from leaving so much ambiguity, but I recall my undergrad being all ambiguity. Indeed, the first two years were a continuous process of "trust us, this will all make sense later," so we had to build our own sense out of things. As a prof, I can't do that now. I am expected to make meaning not just within a course, but within every class / module of the course. I have to signpost every learning goal and every assessment.

The fun lives in the mystery and search for meaning. So does the stress. But that's the deal.

—Kathryn Woodcock, University of Waterloo, Systems Design Engineering

We consider playfulness an attitude, or "a predisposition to define and engage in activities in a nonserious or fanciful manner to increase enjoyment" (Glynn and Webster, 1992, p. 83). This disposition is helpful because people who approach situations with a playful attitude are internally motivated by personal goals and experience an increased focus on active engagement (Glynn and Webster, 1992). Playfulness is no doubt intertwined with the other elements of the Ludic Pedagogy model, yet there is nothing to suggest that a playful attitude cannot be adopted willingly or deliberately. In many cases, a playful attitude is a choice. A conscious decision to embrace a playful attitude can open the individual to experience both fun and a willingness to engage in play. And, as has been seen, interventions can be implemented to stimulate this attitude.

Therefore, even *suggesting* playfulness can have meaningful impacts. If instructors describe that a task or activity is play, such as by saying, "Let's play with this concept," students are more likely to perceive it as less threatening and more experimental. In other words, a more playful attitude can be cultivated simply by suggesting that you'll play with an idea, issue, or problem.

People who are more predisposed to be playful may be more likely to accept this framing, but through encouragement, those less predisposed may be willing to adopt a playful attitude as well. This encouragement may be through explicit discussion of the benefits of playfulness, or simply through modeling it.

Conceptualizing Playfulness

If the idea of playfulness is still too abstract to grasp, or if you are unsure how to embody or otherwise implement it, perhaps a better understanding of its makeup will help. As such, to further describe this element of Ludic Pedagogy and to spark ideas about how to adopt, practice, and model playfulness, this chapter provides an outline of a variety of elements of the concept.

Barnett (1990) identified five constituent dimensions of playfulness: physical spontaneity, social spontaneity, cognitive spontaneity, sense of humor, and manifest joy. The connections between some of these elements to other aspects of the Ludic Pedagogy model are fairly clear. For example, physical spontaneity is related to play, manifest joy to positivity. Barnett's dimensions of playfulness, however, were developed for children; therefore, it may be difficult or inappropriate to generalize this particular conceptualization to students in higher education.

Over a decade later, Barnett (2007) developed a revised definition when examining playfulness in undergraduates: "Playfulness is the predisposition to frame (or reframe) a situation in such a way as to provide oneself (and possibly others) with amusement, humor, and/or entertainment. Individuals who have such a heightened predisposition are typically funny, humorous, spontaneous, unpredictable, impulsive, active, energetic, adventurous, sociable, outgoing, cheerful, and happy, and are likely to manifest playful behavior by joking, teasing, clowning, and acting silly" (p. 955). While helpful to a degree, this definition frames playfulness as a disposition, not an attitude that can be adopted. Interestingly, the same article found no evidence to support the stance that playfulness—in the context of young adults—should be regarded as a trait. In other words, Barnett's research supports this model's conceptualization of playfulness as an attitude, which is nice for two reasons: (1) attitudes can often be more easily adjusted than traits and (2) valuable word count need not be spent refuting it.

Benefits of Playfulness

There is a traditional belief that play only exists on the periphery of adult[6] work, relationships, and, generally speaking, life. In other words, and put very simply, play seems to be for kids (the immature, irresponsible, and uniformed), and seriousness is for adults (who are mature, responsible, and knowledgeable). Proyer (2011) found evidence that this trope is pervasive: playful people tend to perceive themselves as less intelligent than others, perhaps due to the commonly negative connotations associated with nonserious adults. Despite these unfortunate perceptions, there are important benefits to playfulness in education.

One of the most obvious benefits of playfulness in post-secondary education is that greater levels of playfulness are strongly related to higher grades on an exam (Proyer, 2011). Beyond formal assessment via texts and exams, more playful students also demonstrated a greater understanding and retention of material that was not required for the exam. Proyer (2011) argues that these results "might provide ground for future studies in the area of pedagogy and learning studies as fostering playfulness in students or a playful style of learning materials or engaging in exams could positively contribute to their performance" (p. 466). Certainly, increasing interest as evidenced by this book, the number of studies cited, and the resources provided, is a clear indication that playfulness has begun to be more seriously[7] considered an important element in education than it was in the past.

Despite the growing number of studies on playfulness in education, the extent to and means by which playfulness can be incorporated into classroom activities, materials, and assessments is as yet not adequately explored. Furthermore, the level and tone of playfulness required may differ across academic programs, cohorts, ages, or even between different sections of the same course in the same year. The unique combination of instructor characteristics, student characteristics, course content, learning environment, and any number of external factors influence how much and how frequently playfulness is employed. In other words, one cannot rely solely on the literature to help; it is up to the educator to determine what, how, where, and when playfulness should be best implemented.

What does playfulness look like and how does one achieve it? Instructors wishing to develop playfulness in their students can employ many different tools and tactics to encourage the development of a playful attitude. "Playful techniques" refers to teaching methods and approaches to learning that meaningfully incorporate play or elicit playfulness in students.

Whitton (2018) clearly explains:

> Playful tactics are strategies, devices or characteristics that add playfulness into different contexts. They encapsulate playful ways of doing things, elements of playful design or ways of playfully reframing activities or contexts, for example,

by adding elements of humour or silliness (such as throwing a beach ball around a lecture theatre to pick the next student to answer a question), adding chance (using a wheel of fortune to allocate points) or adding elements of novelty or surprise. Using game mechanics in learning contexts, for example, adding competitive aspects, collection of sets or badges, rewards and explicit visible progression, is another set of tactics for potentially adding playfulness to learning. It is important however to be cautious of confusing gamification (the use of game mechanics) with playful learning (a philosophy as well as practice) as the use of the mechanics will not automatically generate a magic circle of play. In some cases, such as the use of competition or leaderboards, these practices may actually have the opposite effect. (p. 6)[8]

But will it work? Yes! Is playfulness just for kids? No! Is playfulness good just for first-year students in higher education? Nope. Glynn and Webster (1992) examined the qualities of playfulness and found that there was no relationship between playfulness and either age or gender. In other words, people do not age out of playfulness. Furthermore, men and women are neither more resistant nor more predisposed to being playful. Playfulness is therefore an all-ages, all-gender inclusive element in Ludic Pedagogy. All are welcome, and the more the merrier.

I was in a class called "Evil in World Religions," which was essentially an analysis of the concept of evil within different cultures and religions around the world.

On the first day of class, our professor walked to the front of the room and put his books down. He stood there looking around at all of us students who were chatting to each other, only half conscious of him, as he hasn't yet started the lecture. He reached over, pulled out a bag of chips and opened it. Still, no one really regarded him too much. He took a chip out of the bag and carefully placed it on the floor. He stood up, looked around, then very obviously reached down, picked the chip up, looked at the class and ate it.

The entire class gave an audible "EWWWW." And he launched into his lecture with, "And why is that gross to you?"

By stimulating a trained response in us, and then having us question it, he connected us with the lecture material. It made us aware that we are a culture with values and norms. It wasn't us just learning about others, it was us learning about ourselves in new and interesting ways.

This fantastic professor never lost anyone's attention, ever.
—C. Bouchard, Student, Bachelor's, University of Manitoba

Playfulness: Humor, Creativity, and Curiosity

The conceptualization of playfulness in the context of Ludic Pedagogy identifies three constituent sub-elements that are of greatest importance to the higher education perspective: humor, creativity, and curiosity. While it may be difficult to envision how to implement the broad scope of playfulness in the classroom, some instructors may find it more feasible to begin to incorporate some of these smaller, more digestible elements. An incremental increase in these sub-elements can increase overall playfulness in the learning environment.

Humor

Humor is an important attitudinal component of Ludic Pedagogy and is tightly interwoven with the purpose and function of the other elements in the model. Being playful, for example, cannot be done effectively without humor. Similarly, students cannot fully engage in play if the opportunity to do so is not presented with humor. Fun is certainly not fun if those engaging in it do not find it amusing.

Once again, however, we find ourselves using an elusive concept.

Ruch (1998) states there exists no general definition of humor. And this is understandable: when considering the highly subjective nature of humor, it is not surprising that a definition is difficult to identify. Indeed, there are so many theories about humor, it isn't funny.[9] Theories of humor, and definitions thereof, originate from a wide range of disciplines—philosophy, psychology, biology, literature—there is likely not a serious[10] field of study that doesn't have a theory on humor.

Even still, we know humor when we see it. For example, when humor is present in class, we know how that feels and how students respond to it. We can sense the feelings and moods evoked by humor, and we can even get a read on people's state of mind based on how they interact with humorous quips, situations, or moments.

Benjelloun (2009) suggests that humor in higher education is "any event that makes the classroom experience pleasant" (p. 313). There is nothing wrong with this definition except for its all-encompassing nature. Any event that makes for a pleasant learning environment is too broad to adequately differentiate it from any of the other core elements in the Ludic Pedagogy model. Fun, play, and playfulness all make the learning experience pleasant, but they're not necessarily humor. At best, this definition underscores the highly interwoven nature of the concepts in Ludic Pedagogy.

The definition of humor as it pertains to Ludic Pedagogy is: the quality of being amusing or comic.[11] But the key element of humor—in the context of pedagogy—is that it is only of value when it aids in learning (Bakar, 2019).

A belief in science allows for a bit of dissection of humor.[12] In doing so, the mechanisms by which humor works can be identified, and how it is—or at very least, can be—effective in the classroom examined. Let's get theoretical.[13]

The Instructional Humor Processing Theory (IHPT) supports the purpose and efficacy of humor in teaching and learning (Wanzer et al, 2010). This theory suggests that humor facilitates learning when the humorous message received by students contains oddness or absurdity. When students perceive something unusual, and then decode or resolve it, they both learn and remember more readily. However, if students fail to perceive or resolve this incongruity, they are less likely to find humor in the message and are more likely to experience confusion. In other words, you can be odd and absurd in your lectures (if that's how you roll), but not so odd and absurd as to confuse your students. The good news is that once students begin to recognize and expect your humorous messaging, their attention will increase (Banas et al, 2011).

According to the IHPT, there are two primary considerations to using humor in the classroom: *relevance* of the humor to the course content, and the humor's *appropriateness*.

It is important that humor in the classroom is relevant so that it does not distract students from the learning process. When humor is indeed relevant, it can make the content more memorable (Banas et al, 2011). In other words, jokes, double-entendres, or wit can serve to make specific information easier to recall or more relatable. Usually, this kind of humor is spontaneous and unexpected. However, irrelevant or even planned humor can actually have a valid and useful place in a classroom. Sometimes, a humorous story, anecdote, or joke that doesn't directly relate to the subject at hand can help to fill time or set a mood. For example, Keith fills silent time—such as when students come into a classroom or enter a Zoom room with microphones off—to make Dad jokes ("Did you hear about the two antennae that got married? The ceremony wasn't that special, but the reception was amazing!"). This kind of groan-y, canned humor does not interrupt or detract from any instructional message and does not violate the principle of appropriateness. In these cases, the humor is in service of the development of a positive, shared environment.[14] On the other hand, interrupting a lecture on a complex topic to tell these same irrelevant jokes could interrupt the learning process, and negatively affect students' comprehension and retention of the material.

This discussion of humor in Ludic Pedagogy is based on the grand assumption that any humor used in class is appropriate. That is, the humor is not discriminatory, racist, sexist, ableist, classist, or offensive to any minoritized group. Such offensive humor, together with targeting students with humor (i.e., teasing), have both been identified by students as being inappropriate (Banas et al, 2011). Negative humor—that which belittles, ridicules, discriminates, or in any way encourages undesirable attitudes or divisiveness within the classroom—is not only problematic, but should be actively discouraged (Chabeli, 2008). Inappropriate or negative humor does not serve Ludic Pedagogy and certainly runs counter to its purposes. If we are to engage students, alienating them through humor diminishes the sense of safety in the classroom which in turn reduces students' willingness to be playful or engage in play. While laughter is important, an overuse of humor or any joke or quip that adversely impacts students' self-esteem or concentration is considered "inappropriate."

Appropriate humor—that which is witty, appropriate, subversive, and does not exclude students—does all kinds of good in the higher education classroom. For example, humor in class can:

- Facilitate learning
- Attract and retain students' attention
- Develop and maintain positive reputation of the instructor
- Enhance the credibility of the instructor
- Build and maintain positive relationship between instructor and students
- Create a pleasant social context
- Build positive attitudes and affect toward learning activities
- Allow instructors to demonstrate positive characteristics such as enthusiasm and passion (Bakar, 2019)
    And finally:
- Humor is kick-ass[15]

There is certainly a whole host of benefits to appropriate humor, but it needs to be made very clear: the Ludic Pedagogy model does not require or even suggest that there is an uninterrupted, direct link between humor and learning. Just because something is funny or entertaining doesn't mean that it will be memorable or meaningful. Wanzer, Frymier, and Irwin (2010) sum up this sentiment by arguing that "just because humor is perceived as appropriate does not necessarily mean that it always increases student learning" (p. 3).

"Appropriate humor" sounds boring, academic-y and, quite frankly, not much fun at all. The phrase feels like a buzzkill. If humor is to be used as a tool in the classroom as part of the Ludic Pedagogy toolbox, then arguably the best term to use is "classroom humor." This term can work under the assumption that those individuals implementing Ludic Pedagogy are, on the whole, a decent group and, by default, not inappropriate.[16]

Humor connects to the core elements of play, playfulness, and fun, and assists in learning. Just as an ace by itself is unlikely to win a hand of poker, that same ace combined with a king, queen, jack, and ten of the same suit is an absolute winner, so it is with humor. Humor is great in and of itself, but it is also enhanced by its coexisting factors.

Nonetheless, the IHPT developed by Wanzer et al (2010) is useful in establishing the forms and functions of humor that are most effective in Ludic Pedagogy. IHPT suggests a process by which students process humorous messages. First, students must recognize any humor in the instructor's communication. Second, the humorous message must be deciphered. Third, messages must be evaluated in terms of (1) the affect elicited—positive or negative—and (2) if they help in processing or understanding the course content. Smiles and laughter are the key indications that messages have been received, interpreted, and if they stimulated positive affect. The IHPT model then proposes that the positive affect heightens motivation to process, leading to increased learning. Ludic Pedagogy suggests that playfulness, play, and fun act as intervening variables in this process.

Because humorous messages need to be interpreted, the wide range of personal and cultural experiences that exist in many classrooms today can therefore make the use of humor challenging. The "individual differences of sex, teaching experience and acclaim, humor orientation, immediacy, and culture" (Banas et al, 2011, p. 125) affect the efficacy of humor in educational settings. However, there are useful learning implications of humor. Because some people may find something in the classroom funny and others do not, this discrepancy promotes and encourages the development of both critical thinking and emotional intelligence. Obviously, there are a great number of variables to keep in mind when attempting to utilize humor. Courage is needed, as using humor as a tool is bound to fail at one point or another. Bombing "on stage" cannot be allowed to derail the focus of the engagement with students: their learning.[17]

In more practical terms, humor in the classroom helps the instructor indicate that teaching and learning is not a chore. There can exist levity, lightness, and delight involved in approaching the unknown or tackling a difficult problem. Humor engages the student. It can surprise and cue new ways of thinking.

While some authors (Bolkan et al, 2018, for example) suggest that humor may serve as a distractor in the classroom in terms of direct learning, they also acknowledge the positive impact that humor can have on developing a positive environment, which in turn increases motivation. This disconnect once again highlights the importance of considering the entire Ludic Pedagogy model rather than traditional silos of study. Whereas Bolkan et al (2018) state that "instructors should be careful not to integrate humor in a manner that competes for students' attention" (p. 158), the integration of humor via Ludic Pedagogy may serve to help reduce cognitive load and can increase both comprehension and retention.

Humor can help develop a relationship between instructors and students by reducing the psychological distance between the two (Wanzer et al, 2010). In a study by Aylor and Opplinger (2003), students who believed their instructor to be high in humor orientation were more likely to seek out their instructors and communicate with them outside of class. Furthermore, students of faculty with a high orientation to humor were more likely to discuss their personal problems with their instructors, find their outside-of-class communications to be more satisfactory, and believe their relationships with instructors to be more meaningful. All these benefits sound beneficial and appear to be a huge endorsement for the use of humor, but this personal style characterized by close relationships may not suit all instructors. Thus, the use of humor should be deliberate according to the instructor's personal style and intended level of contact with students.

The incorporation of humor can help to craft the instructor's desired learning environment and can serve a range of purposes. For example, high levels of humor can develop a sense of cohesion through the creation of a positive, shared, enjoyable environment. Humor can also aid instruction by softening criticism (Banas et al, 2011). The demonstration of a humorous attitude on the part of the instructor[18] can demonstrate an expression of divergent thinking, which encourages more open and transparent interaction within the classroom. The shared laughter which is a product of humor may also serve to increase group cohesiveness and, therefore, reduce students' social anxiety, again improving classroom interactions and communication (Ziv, 1976).

Literature has established that humor promotes learning through a positive, affective, psychosocial learning environment. However, there is less evidence that humor directly impacts learning itself: "Despite the fact that humor is an effective means of gaining attention, empirical evidence is less favorable regarding the positive effects of humor on information acquisition and retention" (Banas et al, 2012, p. 132). This lack of evidence illustrates the importance of embracing all of the elements of Ludic Pedagogy—humor is not the be-all and end-all. Humor is simply part of playfulness which is only one element used to support our students.

"But I'm not, by nature, a humorous person! This is impossible!" says someone reading this chapter. Nonsense.

Provine (2000) in *Laughter: A Scientific Investigation*, provides some simple guidelines for increasing humor in your own life,[19] including:

1. Create a casual and safe environment;
2. Adopt a laugh-ready attitude;
3. Provide humorous materials; and
4. Eliminate social inhibitions.

The first three points seem easy enough, but "eliminate social inhibitions"? How do I do that? Put a little whiskey in my coffee cup? You do what works for you, but there is no need to resort to the use of liquid courage. Like the rest of this chapter, the focus is on your attitude: being brave, being willing to look silly, positive risk-taking, and the like. Who cares if you fumble once or twice in the classroom? Students will remember it and, just perhaps, the concept you were attempting to convey. At the risk of stating the obvious, you are the expert in the room—use that power and feel free, on occasion, to make a bit of a fool of yourself. In short, relax. Have fun. Life's too short to do otherwise.

A more relaxed atmosphere that promotes laughter can be invoked by employing a careful and considerate use of humor in the post-secondary classroom. A positive learning environment can also be enhanced when students accept and even reciprocate the use of humor. Such an environment encourages students to express more freedom and to do so in less conventional ways—in ways that illustrate divergent thinking "not bound to 'right' [. . .] answers" (Ziv, 1976, p. 320).

This potential for divergent thinking leads us to the next element of playfulness: creativity.

Creativity

Often, creativity is a trait we want to encourage and develop in our students. Bateson and Nettle (2014) define creativity as "when an individual develops a novel form of behaviour or a novel idea, regardless of its practical uptake and subsequent application" (p. 221).

Playfulness both relies on and encourages creativity. That is, the two exist in a real chicken-and-egg kind of relationship: being playful means being creative and, often, being creative means being playful in terms of imagination. Adopting a playful attitude allows students (and faculty, for that matter) to step outside the day-to-day reality of their lives and look beyond what is normally perceived as their limitations. As noted by Ziv (1976) playfulness can lead to divergent thinking, and can help students find answers and outcomes that they would be far less likely to reach through conventional thinking. Given that we want students to play with ideas and concepts in order to better understand and retain them, creativity is therefore an integral element of playfulness. In addition, by engaging with different experiences and discounting what would normally be seen as boundaries, playfulness encourages and facilitates creativity (Bateson & Nettle, 2014).[20]

Put simply, playfulness and creativity are reciprocal concepts. If one is creative, they are almost certainly playful. In turn, one who is playful will often exhibit characteristics of creativity. Chang (2013) argues that playfulness is a direct predictor of student creativity. While research has not made it clear which comes first, there exists a valid relationship between playfulness and creativity (Bateson & Nettle, 2014).

Opening possibilities for creativity and playfulness is easier than one may think—and *way* more fun that any "rigor-only" scholar could imagine.

Most courses culminate in a specific paper, essay, or exam. But Sharon decided to buck this trend by presenting students in each of her courses with the freedom to devise, create, and submit their own final projects in ways that they want, need, or desire. First, she asks students to choose their own specific project topics—something derived from the breadth of issues addressed in class. The topic can be something that they find interesting, compelling, controversial, or that they are quite simply curious about. After she approves the topic and its parameters, students are invited to research, practice, or organize their project and present it in a way that "fits" with the project or plays to their strengths.

That is absolutely a wide-open door. But don't worry, presenting students with freedom and choice is not terrifying, disorganized, or elusive. And it won't totally mess with your assessment/grading/marking/evaluation.

Such an unrestricted and creative assignment is sometimes called an "unessay." The term "unessay" is somewhat problematic in that it defines itself by what it is not, but the authors of this book didn't make up that name.[21] The apparent earliest reference to an unessay is from Daniel Paul O'Donnell (2012) of University of Lethbridge. O'Donnell describes an essay (which is derived from the French word meaning "trial") as constricting and a "rule-bound monster." Rather, O'Donnell invited his students to throw out the rules that they learned to date, focus on their own intellectual interests, and present their work in a compelling and/or creative way. Put simply, he invited students to create a summative project by: (1) choosing their own topic, (2) presenting it any way they please, and (3) evaluating students on the compelling nature and efficacy of their arguments and presentations. Similarly, Emily Suzanne Clark (2016) invites students to respond to a final paper prompt by choosing to write either a traditional essay or an unessay.

When given the freedom to be creative beyond the confines of a traditional paper, essay, or exam, students produce remarkable work. For example, two students in Sharon's Communication and Conflict course started an Instagram account that featured university students, faculty, and staff on campus, much like Humans of New York (See figure 3.1). This account was a communicative gesture toward connection. Another student who had previously enjoyed painting and drawing but hadn't had the opportunity to use this skill once entering university produced a series of artwork honoring her brother who struggled with drug addiction and the conflicts that the family overcame (figure 3.2). The student provided an artist's statement that outlined how communication was fundamental to her family's healing, and her art was a form of expressive communication. One foodie used new recipes that she tried and then delivered to friends and family as a communicative device to express gratitude (figure 3.3). Others made podcasts, vlogs, websites, or started a novel-length book. All projects were built upon theoretical concepts addressed in the course, together with personal experience and secondary or primary research. The most important element of the project is always creativity.

Like O'Donnell (2012), Sharon found that students appreciate the "real" nature of the unessay assignments. That is, they have a much clearer understanding of how course concepts connect to their own interests, skills, and ideas. Many of the projects that students do are experiments—some of which come out the way they anticipated, and others, well, not so much. And there's value there, too. The bonus of the unessay for instructors is that they are super fun to assess. Sure, Sharon constructs a rubric with her students each term—criteria can include levels of commitment, how compelling is the presentation, how well the project connects to course concepts, and so on. But the real joy is in seeing students enjoy the freedom of creativity, and not having to read the same essay topic sixty-five times. When end-of-term grading time comes around, assessing unessays and projects of this sort are usually downright enjoyable.

Figure 3.1 Student Work Example. *Source:* Roger Ragoonath and Matthew Wilson.

Figure 3.2 Student Work Example. *Source*: **Kayla Cook.**

Curiosity

Physicist, pacifist, and Nobel Prize winner Albert Einstein claimed that he was neither clever nor gifted, but, rather, was "passionately curious." Curious can mean eager to know or learn something, but it can also mean that something is unusual or strange. In the context of Ludic Pedagogy, the qualities of being inquisitive, analytical, exploratory, and interested are valued. When discussing curiosity, a quality of playfulness is again being addressed, as Pichlmair (2009) argues that "Playfulness is an attitude of exploration" (p. 252).

Curiosity can certainly exist independently of playfulness—consider a scientist driven by curiosity to continue experiment after experiment in order to find an answer or solution. Such experiments may not be playful, but they can certainly be driven by curiosity. However, there is a clear relationship

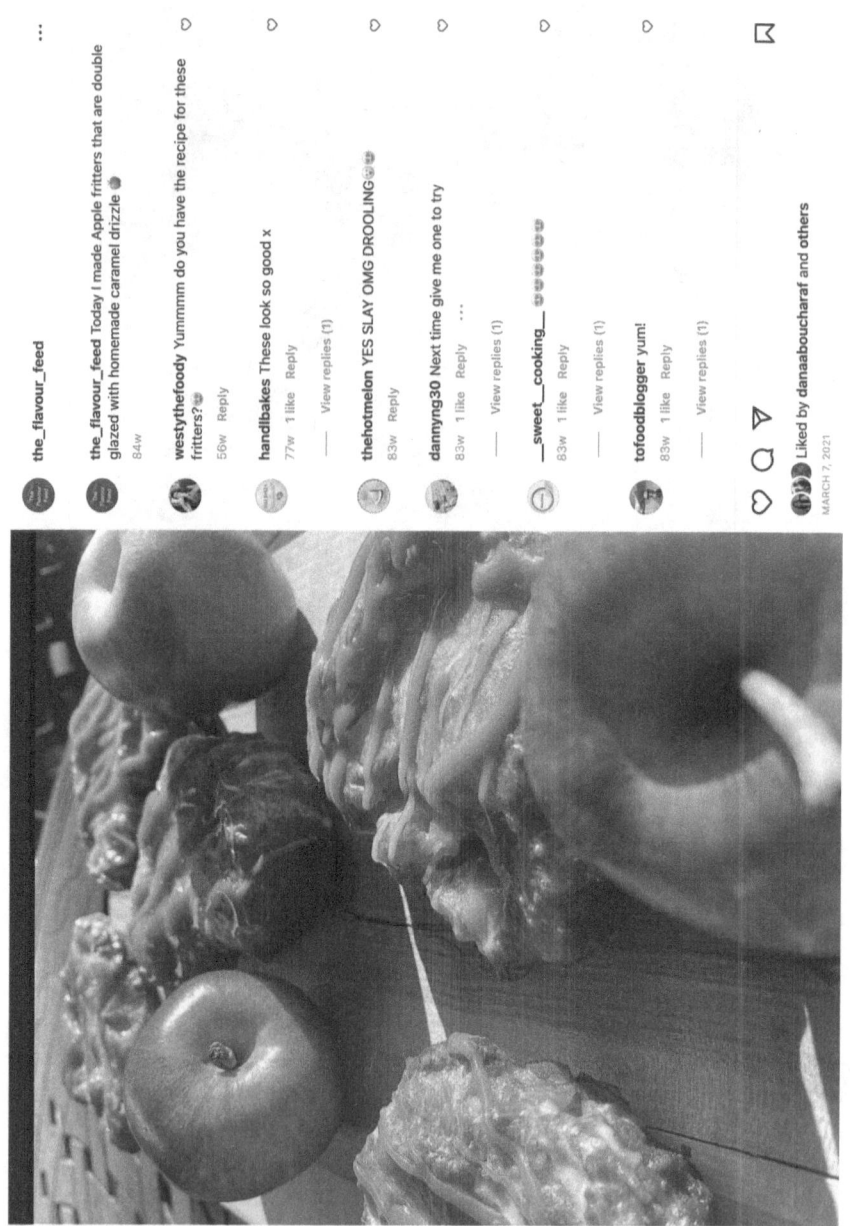

Figure 3.3 Student Work Example. *Source:* Breanna Ng.

between playfulness and curiosity, for playfulness can be used to arouse curiosity. Curiosity is thus part and parcel of playfulness: just as playfulness drives creativity, it cannot exist without curiosity. Playful people want to try new things, explore possibilities, and do all the things that are motivated by curiosity.

> Dr. Victoria Kannen of Laurentian University in Sudbury has developed an engaging exercise that encourages students to question how language and ideas are often taken for granted. She asks the students to collectively come up with a definition of what a "chair" is. After deciding on the parameters of what a chair might be—this can often be joyfully contentious—she then asks them to do the same for "table." What follows is a series of images for which the students are asked to decide whether it is a chair or table. The images begin rather simply but progress into more modern, abstract, and obfuscated notions of these two simple objects. The activity ends with the sneaky introduction of a modern art piece that is neither table nor chair—but could have elements of either, or both. After disclosing to the students that the final image was technically neither table nor chair, Victoria explains the purpose of the activity—to introduce the idea that definitions, ideas, and theories, that may seem rigid and fixed, can often be reimagined and fluid when questioned. This exercise demonstrates how an idea or object students would—at the beginning of the exercise—dismiss as a commonplace item became theoretically possible as "table" or "chair" within their broadened ideas of what they now could be.
> —Victoria Kannen, Faculty, Laurentian University

Dubey et al (2021) showed that curiosity can be enhanced by external forces, such as a learner's social environment. Therefore, instructors who can successfully modify the social context of the classroom to be playful—that is, develop a class-wide attitude of playfulness—will likely be able to excite greater curiosity[22] among their students. When curiosity is further aligned with the intrinsic motivator of fun, there is no end to the good stuff that could happen, including even winning the authors of this book a Nobel Prize.

Curiosity, like creativity, is both an element of playfulness (i.e., it is part of what makes playfulness thrive) and is stimulated by it (i.e., playfulness invokes curiosity). That is, it is entirely unclear which comes first—the curiosity or the playfulness. Research shows, however, that the two have a clear and symbiotic relationship. Dubey et al (2021) showed the relative ease by which the curiosity of participants in classroom activities could be influenced. In their experiment, the authors showed participants common questions about science, each of the questions accompanied by the number of "up-votes" the questions had received from an online forum. The number of up-votes was used as a social clue to popularity. A low number of up-votes reduced curiosity more so than a high number of up-votes increased curiosity. Surprise mediated these effects. Using these findings, we see that curiosity can be manipulated using surprise and perceived popularity. And the use of playfulness, in most cases, is also likely to arouse curiosity in even moderately engaged students.

Curiosity in the classroom can be easily implemented by introducing a relevant case study or anecdote at the beginning of a lesson. Much like a movie or television show that begins in the middle of the story, the audience (students) are drawn into the narrative. Once hooked, the instructor can engage in a "flashback," introducing the topic for the lesson and working forward to the point that began the class.

For example, Sharon incorporates a study of the Heinz Dilemma in her third-year Communication Ethics course. She begins by introducing a hypothetical situation in which Mr. Heinz's wife is dying of a rare type of cancer. The drug company has a cure, but the cost of the drug is beyond Mr. Heinz's means, even after he canvasses friends and family for donations, and even after he begs the pharmaceutical CEO for an exemption. Heinz then must decide: Does he steal the drug for his dying wife? Students are very curious about this dilemma: What would happen to Mr. Heinz's wife if he were put in prison for the crime? What should happen if Mr. Heinz didn't really love his wife? Why is the price of the drug so high? Although this is a developmental psychology question, the ethics course begs curious questions of students well beyond psychological development and extends into economics, sociology, and medicine.

Let's face it, curiosity is likely what brings students to our classrooms. The course description sounds cool, the program is interesting, and the problems in the discipline are important to solve. Thus, faculty should not ignore the power of student curiosity. After all, it is what gets students enrolled and what keeps them at our universities. Similarly, instructors ought not dismiss the role they play in the cultivation and proliferation of the beneficial quality of curiosity: teachers have a much greater impact on student curiosity—and resultant exploration and learning—than do family members or peers (Inyat & Ali, 2020).

Strictly speaking, our job is only to help students obtain knowledge in our courses. Yet ideally, we want to foster in them a curiosity that will transcend our classrooms and drive these students into the future. We want them to be curious. We want them to learn more than what we have to offer. As Walt Disney purportedly[23] said, "We keep moving forward, opening new doors, and doing new things, because we're curious and curiosity keeps leading us down new paths."

Conclusion

Playfulness is an attitude that encapsulates a range of concepts including creativity, curiosity, and sense of humor. Beyond the positive role of playfulness in the learning process, helping students develop this attitude is a life skill that will serve them well in any personal or professional activity they undertake. To do this, educators need to embody playfulness and its constituent elements.

Playfulness is good. Full stop.

As stated by Yip and Martin (2006), "Individuals with a more playful, less serious attitude toward life appear to be better able to strike up conversations and initiate friendships with others, perhaps because of a greater willingness to take interpersonal risks in a playful way" (p. 1207). In the classroom, these interpersonal risks between students and between students and their instructor can lead to a greater sense of trust and, therefore, a greater willingness to engage in classroom activities and discourse. The outcome is, again, heightened learning.

CHAPTER 4

Positivity

The sounds of an ice-cream truck are unmistakable. Whether it's a crowded beach or busy neighborhood, kids will drop their toys and sprint to the next stop when they hear the familiar jingle. And rightly so, it's hard to be in a bad mood when the ice-cream truck arrives. There is quite possibly joy infused into an ice-cream sandwich, popsicle, or dessert bar (and hooray, Gen Z is bringing Viennetta back to popularity). Indeed, the ice-cream brand Good Humor got its name from the belief that one's "humor"—or one's mood or state of mind—came from the humor of the palate. It's a traditional belief that good-tasting food results in a positive temperament (Unilever, 2021).[1]

While dining halls might host "make your own sundae" nights, ice cream rarely makes an appearance in the higher-education classroom. But the metaphor holds true: the intake of positive inputs can—and does—lead to positive affect. Hanging out with positive people, ideas, and overall vibes are likely to lead to more of the same, but a little ice cream never hurts.

Positivity as Affect

Positivity is the *affect* element of Ludic Pedagogy. The moods and emotions that we invoke as instructors, and that students experience, are fundamental to this teaching framework. While recognizing that there is a wealth of research on affect and emotions,[2] this book is not going to attempt to write a primer on this material here. Very generally speaking, affect is that thing that underlies emotion, good or bad. With apologies to those who spend their careers studying and writing about these issues, this book will conflate terms of affect, emotion, and mood, though each means something slightly different. The intention is not to muddy the waters of the topic of affect, but instead to use common language that is accessible to all readers. Academics who take exception—contact the authors. There's a collaboration to be found there!

As instructors, we want students to feel happy, satisfied, and/or content with their learning experiences. These are obvious examples of positive affect. By contrast, we want to reduce negative emotions such as aggression, anger, or anxiety as they represent negative affect (Pekrun, 2011). Kay, Banks, and Craig (2021) found that students reported happiness as the emotion most often expressed when learning, followed by anxiety, sadness, and anger. Clearly, the desire is to maximize positive emotions relative to learning. A focus on positivity is of particular importance given that three of the top four emotions that students reported relative to their learning were negative.

Despite the desire for happy students, positivity as envisioned in this model also encapsulates optimism, enthusiasm, confidence, patience, and integrity. When students approach coursework with this mindset, it becomes possible to engage with course topics in constructive ways, and to do so even when issues addressed are difficult or serious. Positivity does not refer to blind joyfulness, regardless of context. For example, it is both inadvisable and difficult to approach studies of the Holocaust, war, colonization, violence, or misogyny with "joyfulness." Rather, the Ludic Pedagogy conceptualization of positivity in learning means that students can take on learning—even about challenging subjects—with a sense of curiosity, inquisitiveness, and with a solution-oriented attitude.

Toxic positivity is a dangerous prospect and deserves the kind of attention it won't receive here. The Ludic Pedagogy model is not suggesting that positive emotions (again, such as happiness) are required no matter how dire or difficult a situation is. Faculty are not cheerleaders and neither are students (unless they have purposefully tried out for a team, and then by all means, they are bona fide cheerleaders). There are bound to be situations in learning that are frustrating, annoying, or demanding. Yet it is possible for instructors to approach teaching with the objective to increase student motivation and engagement. So too is it possible for students to experience the benefits of learning so that they feel good about a course, assignment, or concept. The traits of positivity as outlined in this model can give rise to happiness, excitement, and satisfaction, but they are not the core ideals upon which to focus.

There's an illustrative positivity scenario in *The Chair*, the Netflix comedy/drama released in 2021: Professor Yaz McKay (Nana Mensah) is a young faculty member in the English department at Pembroke University (a liberal arts college, probably in New England) who is up for tenure. She is unlike the stale, pale, male senior faculty members who lecture to half-asleep students. In her classes, students talk to one another and to Dr. McKay. They ask questions. They act out scenes from plays and novels. The students are engaged—they understand, debate, and think. The series depicts the differences between the vibrancy evident in Dr. McKay's classes and the drudgery and boredom in senior faculty's classrooms. Twitter was alight with academics expressing sentiments about the accuracy of the series—because the contrast between Dr. McKay's courses and those of the faculty past their best-by date was obvious. It is the positivity evoked by both Dr. McKay and her students that is the goal.

Positivity and Motivation and Cognitive Functioning, Oh My!

Positivity has the potential to make a significant impact on student motivation. For example, Craig et al (2004) suggest that one's affective state (that is, mood and emotion) is connected to one's degree of motivation. Intrinsic motivation is paramount: when someone wants to learn or complete a task, motivation that arises from within the individual is much more effective than that due to external motivators. Learners who are both intrinsically motivated and affectively engaged are likely to be more involved and persistent in their tasks.

Of course, positive emotions also have an impact on external motivators—feeling good can affect results such as validation or acknowledgment from other people. When external motivators are in the context of academic performance—that is, when a student feels positive about grades, awards, and validation or praise from an instructor, the impact increases as well (Wu et al, 2021). However, the focus of this model is on intrinsic motivation (see Chapter 1, Fun) because when one is motivated from within, they are more likely to have a changed perception of themselves and will thus be more likely to change their behavior (Clanton Harpine, 2015).

In an academic setting, positive affect has a significant role to play: positive emotions can create higher levels of academic engagement, intrinsic motivation, self-efficacy, self-regulation, and achievement (Datu et al, 2017). As educators, we want our students to not only understand the subjects that we teach but also to have cultivated an internal drive and emotional well-being. If we want students to learn how to learn, want to learn, and feel good about learning (and themselves), then the fundamental issues of motivation and affect cannot be ignored (Linnenbrink, 2007).

> The best experience I had in college was working on a final business project. This experience is memorable because of both the positive interactions that I had while working with fellow classmates and the knowledge that we were able to pull from the instructors leading the class. The instructors were very knowledgeable in a variety of industries and they were very good at helping us to think outside of the box on our projects. The whole experience felt very collaborative and it was clear that the instructors genuinely wanted to help us. This final assignment served as a valuable experience for me because of the resources and skills I developed while creating our business. Now that I have started working, I still refer back to the skills that I gained from my classmates and instructors while doing this major project.
> —Justin Demers, Diploma, Assiniboine Community College

Research on affect and learning indicates that emotions can affect effort, motivation to persist, learning strategies, and cognitive concepts—even if the student is unaware of the effects at the time. Pekrun's (2011) cognitive/motivational model of affect (the grouping of emotions based on valence and activation) shows that feelings and emotions can influence cognitive processes that underpin human learning. These thought processes include "(1) attention and memory processes; (2) motivation to learn; (3) use of learning strategies; and (4) self-regulation of learning" (p. 26). This study suggests that one's emotional state, the learning environment, and the affect of a learning group will impact how one thinks and how well they learn.

Approaching or Avoiding Learning
Another[3] way of understanding the relationship between positive affect and student motivation is Linnenbrink's (2007) suggestion that individuals—in this case, students—who experience positive affect are more likely to adopt an "approach" stance to a task rather than an "avoid" one. The idea is that students experiencing positive affect are more likely to perceive that they have the knowledge, skills, abilities, or whatever other resources are required to engage with a task or to illustrate their competence for engaging in a task. Students who do not experience positive affect, and instead are steeped in negative affect, will instead adopt an avoidance strategy in an attempt to

negate an unwanted outcome. That is, students with positive affect are more willing to *try*, while those students not experiencing the same sort of affect are more apt to try simply to *avoid* failure.

The concept of positive affect and effort can be illustrated in an example that many of us don't even have to "imagine": Let's say that a student is enrolled in two classes. In one class, the professor makes learning enjoyable by showing enthusiasm, empathy, good humor, and happiness—you get the vibe. The course material may even be somewhat uninspiring,[4] but the experience of going to class creates at the very least a *somewhat* positive affective experience for this imaginary student. Their second class, despite the student's interest in the subject matter, is frightfully dull. The professor speaks in a monotone, is not interested in students' input, and generally elicits no emotion at all. Here, the student finds boredom. In this example, the student is likely to adopt an *approach* strategy to the class in which they experience positive affect and an *avoidance* strategy in the class in which they experience negative affect.

Learning and Grades
Beyond issues of motivation, research shows that positivity has such an effect on learning by specifically impacting cognitive processes that allow for effective learning including information processing, communication processing, negotiation processing, decision-making, and creative problem-solving (Um et al, 2011). Not only are these cognitive processes heightened, but research also suggests that due to positive affect, many of these cognitive processes are more flexible, which may result in greater levels of creativity and ability to problem-solve (Isen et al, 1987). Conversely, negative emotions (such as anxiety) have an adverse effect on learning by consuming cognitive resources and redirecting attention away from the learning itself (Zeidner, 1998). In other words, students who are in a positive frame of mind learn better in a whole range of ways. As the people charged with helping students learn, it therefore falls to us to help them approach their courses and course content in a positive state of mind.

Connections among positivity, improved cognitive functioning, and post-secondary success are clear. An extensive literature review examining more than twenty-five studies from a range of disciplines demonstrated that positive affect enhances learners' cognitive flexibility, ability to identify alternative perspectives, creative problem-solving skills, and other important learning abilities (Ashby et al, 1999). These findings have only been further supported and expanded upon in the twenty years since this comprehensive review.

Much less clear, however, is the connection between affect and grades that students receive in post-secondary education; some studies indicate a positive relationship between grades and positive affect, while other studies indicate a negative relationship, and still others have no correlations at all (Nickerson et al, 2010). In an attempt to clarify these inconsistent findings, some researchers have considered emotions while learning. "Academic emotions" is the term used to define affect that is directly tied to teaching, learning, and academic achievement in both informal and formal education contexts (Um et al, 2011). Applying this concept in terms of higher education students, not only do positive emotions have positive effects on students adopting learning goals, but negative (unpleasant) emotions have negative effects. These same results also hold true with those emotions arising from learning achievements: positive emotions such as happiness, enjoyment, and pride have positive impacts on ongoing motivation, whereas negative emotions such as anger, shame, and anxiety are negatively related to the same motivational factors (Pekrun, 2011).

It becomes increasingly obvious that faculty need to help students have a positive outlook on their educational activities so that they can develop, maintain, and enhance their motivation and learning abilities. The importance of a positive outlook may mean that we all need to work to destigmatize situations in which a student does not meet the level of outcome that they expected (which, admittedly, sounds like a euphemism for "when a student fails"). When a student doesn't get the grade that they want or expect, or if they struggle more than they anticipated, they should not necessarily be deemed a failure if they have applied themselves and engaged in the activity or assessment. Rather, falling short can be considered an opportunity to identify areas where efforts should be focused. Alternative grading methods are another way to flip the script to help maintain students' positive affect (see Chapter 6, Implementation and Impacts).

Emotional Overload!
Dropping the bomb that instructors ought to be mindful of students' emotions while learning will not come without resistance.

"That's not why I have a PhD!"
"It's not my job to coddle these kids!"
"I'm here to help them learn to think! Feelings have nothing to do with it."

Certainly, few graduate programs teach PhD students how to teach, and even fewer (maybe even none!) address the importance of student emotions while teaching in higher education.

Yet awareness and care for emotions have the potential to significantly transform students' learning experiences. One doesn't have to get all warm and fuzzy to recognize this, and it certainly doesn't mean that students and faculty need to be hanging out by the campfire singing *Kumbaya* each and every day. It just means that we are aware of both where students are at, emotionally speaking, and how our teaching can affect them. Are students in, as Ron Burgundy exclaims in *Anchorman*, "a glass case of emotion"?[5] If so, how do we meet them there or coax them out? Further, is it the teaching itself that is putting students in that glass case of emotion? Let's hope not, and make sure that students are kept where the air is fresh.

The bottom line here is that learning is not separate from emoting. The two phenomena are better envisioned as interdependent and somewhat overlapping in nature (Oliver et al, 2010). In other words, when one learns, one also experiences emotions. Learning can make someone feel happy, excited, or overwhelmed. Emotions—whether positive or negative—can affect how well, quickly, or thoroughly one learns. These emotions may be present before the student even walks in the door or logs into a virtual classroom (think of the fear, anxiety, and insecurity when students were learning online during the height of COVID). While there is little control to be had over the timing of global pandemics, what *can* be controlled is the tone and pace of one's teaching, because it directly affects students' emotions. And these emotions affect their learning.

Emotion plays a variety of roles relative to cognitive load. Emotions can produce extra mental load (i.e., more things to think about, manage, and balance) and can be an additional component to process while learning (Lawson et al, 2021). Affect, then, can have a meaningful impact on one's capacity for cognitive activities. Some emotional states (anxiety, for example) may be deemed disruptive because of the task-irrelevant thinking that arises from the state of being anxious ("OMG I totally don't understand this, I'm gonna fail, and if I fail, I won't get a job, and if I don't get a job, I won't have any money, and if I don't have any money, I'll be homeless, and if I'm homeless . . . ").[6] These anxious thoughts decrease the available cognitive capacity that would otherwise be used when engaging in an academic task (Um et al, 2011).

Great! Let's keep our students overjoyed with their learning and the problem is solved!

Like most things academic, it's not that simple.

It's not just negative emotions that can cause extraneous cognitive loads—both positive and negative emotions can have this taxing effect. Positive emotions, if strong enough, can also lead to disruptive thinking and, therefore, extraneous cognitive load! For example, if a student is super-excited about Linear Algebra,[7] or if class activities are so much fun that they become like the Heaven and Hell frat party last weekend, there is just too much to process. In turn, the diminished cognitive resources available to the student will lead to decreased learning, lower satisfaction with their learning, and a lower perception of what they actually learned (Um et al, 2011). In other words, under the extraneous cognitive load theory, strong enough emotions—whether positive or negative—will have a negative impact on the student's ability to learn.

It's like salt in food—some is good. Too much ruins it.

To continue this spicy learning metaphor,[8] emotions and cognition are found together like salt and pepper. As students are exposed to new information and try to make sense of these new ideas and concepts, they are almost certainly going to have an emotional experience (Stein & Levine, 1991). This affect may be positive (wonder, excitement, interest) or it may be negative (boredom, disgust, frustration). In either case, when new information or ideas are presented to students, the autonomic nervous system is aroused. This stimulation, coupled with a requisite cognitive activity, creates an emotional reaction. Therefore, learning most often occurs during an emotional experience (Craig et al, 2004). Given that emotions are going to be part of learning and student engagement anyway, let's work with them in the most productive way possible.

The Positivity of Negative Affect

When most people think of negative affect, they conjure up situations full of complaints, resistance, anger, arguments, or even feelings such as boredom or laziness. Negativity feels unpleasant and most will want to avoid it. But again, the situation isn't so simple. Negativity may have some redeeming factors.

Empirical studies have often found that negative emotions (such as anger, shame, and boredom) are generally associated with task-irrelevant thinking and reduced learning in higher education (Pekrun, 2011). However, negative affect has also been positively associated with focused, detail-oriented, and analytical methods of thinking (Clore & Huntsinger, 2007). A simple example would be a student frustrated with learning a statistical method. The student may become intently focused on the step-by-step application of a particular formula, equation, or mathematical tool. Such concentrated attention is likely to have a positive impact on this student's learning, even though it was caused by the negative affect of frustration.

Positivity, then, can be recast to consider not only a focus on positive affect, but also the potential for positive outcomes resulting from experiencing negative affect. That is, under some learning conditions, such as when a student has plenty of time, a supportive group of colleagues, a helpful instructor, and/or purposeful tutorials, negative affect (such as frustration, anxiety, impatience) can serve a positive purpose. The student is pushed beyond their previous boundaries and therefore can develop coping strategies, new knowledge, or improved understanding.

Both students and instructors can orient emotions—either positive or negative—in productive ways. Rather than students avoiding class or not completing coursework, negative affect should be channeled so that it helps students to develop good habits such as focusing on the details of assignments, careful studying, or diligent editing.

Source of Positivity

There are two aspects of positivity that are most important in understanding—and cultivating—positive affect relative to learning: (1) the learner's felt emotion during learning, and (2) the instructor's portrayed emotion during instruction (Lawson et al, 2021). The two phenomena are closely related.

Under optimal conditions, when students receive instruction or engage in a learning task, they feel some sort of positive affect such as excitement (Buff et al, 2011). In other words, there is often a correlation between a student's engagement with learning and their experience of positive affect. As might be expected, engagement or commitment to learning can lead to an upward spiral in such a situation—students who experience happiness or some other sort of positive affect are more likely to seek similar positive educational experiences, which will lead to further instances of positive affect (Stiglbauer et al, 2013). "That was a cool activity," a student may think after class. "I'm not going to miss next week's class. I'll go back to see if we're doing something else that's fun/meaningful/helpful/engaging next week."

Simply stated, the students who have positive emotional experiences in their learning are more likely to exert greater amounts of effort, demonstrate the positive affect that they experience, and more effectively use their cognitive resources when engaging with academic tasks (Datu et al, 2017). In other words, it is those students who find learning fun—and are therefore intrinsically motivated—who will be engaged with learning experiences. It therefore follows that if learning tasks are fun, enjoyable, or engaging, students are more likely to experience positive affect when participating in them, and thus experience increased motivation.

Assessment

Students are more likely to enjoy class when they perceive learning activities as valuable and something over which they have control. That is, when course content is seen as interesting and/or useful and as something over which the student believes they can develop some degree of mastery, they are more likely to enjoy it. On the other hand, if the student perceives the course materials or content as lacking in value, they are likely to experience negative affect, and, put simply, care very little about the assignment and the potential learning therein. They'll just do the assignment to do it and get it over and done. Students motivated to simply avoid failure are more likely to engage in behaviors of questionable academic integrity, rather than through more positive, desirable academic behaviors (Pekrun, 2011).

The element of control is particularly important in terms of assessments. Most traditional assignments include essays, tests, quizzes, presentations, papers, or lab reports. Students will complete the assignment, submit it to the instructor, and only those few parties (and maybe a teaching assistant) will ever see it. The assignment stays in the course learning management system or gets recycled if it is printed. Students see little value in these assignments. They are literally disposable. Once the student completes them and the instructor marks them, they're tossed. Students feel like the lowly trash panda—cute, stays up all night, and gets by on garbage.[9]

Further to the perceived value of an assignment, Pekrun (2011) outlines two aspects of assessment that can lead to the arousal of student emotions: (1) the feedback students receive on their assessments; and (2) the students' perceived consequences of success and failure on an assessment.

Feedback is fundamental to student success, and an increasing body of literature outlines the importance of fair and formative feedback (see Lauricella and Kay, 2022 for review). Good feedback will tell a student how well they are progressing on expectations for an assignment or in a course (Feldman, 2019), and will give them suggestions and guidance on how they can improve going forward (Talbert, 2015). It should be sensitive to the individual needs of the student and ought to focus on what the student is doing well or right (Reynolds, 2022). Sharon experimented with audio feedback in some of her courses with great success. While research shows that students like receiving audio feedback from instructors because it is helpful and clear (Brearley & Cullen, 2015), Sharon's students reported that audio feedback felt more authentic. One student said that when she reads a professor's written comments on her academic work, she hears them in a "mean voice," but audio feedback is helpful because it can more clearly show if the instructor is making a sincere effort to be helpful and constructive. The emotional impact of audio/visual feedback is significant and deserves future attention in scholarly research.

Students are busy, stressed, and must prioritize all the stuff happening in their lives. Sometimes they just can't do it all (or they just don't feel like doing it all, which is also fair—they're human). Even arts students have done the math to figure out, "What happens if I don't submit this?" Beyond the quantitative, students can also weigh how the instructor might perceive them, or how the assignment might contribute to a larger, scaffolded submission later. If students see a connection between their own success and desirable outcomes—such as a good grade, favorable perceptions, or the potential impact of their work—positive emotions (such as hope or excitement) may increase. On the other hand, if students perceive negative consequences of failure (such as a bad grade or actual, legitimate failure, collapse of future assignments, or significant disorganization) negative emotions (such as anxiety or hopelessness) may result.

While negative affect has its purpose and it is good to run away from fire, too much anxiety and bathing in stress-induced cortisol is no way to live. Effective teaching means that we need to think about our students' emotions. It doesn't mean that a customer service department needs to be established with the aim of making them "happy," but it does mean that faculty can work to encourage a positive, productive affect.

Because a student will receive a grade at the end of their course, they believe every assessment plays a significant role in their eventual success or failure. In most academic institutions, a grade has a variety of ranks associated with passing (A–D), and one with failure (F). Grades hold a variety of inherent challenges, the most glaring of which is that grades do not equal feedback: simply providing a grade to a student tells them very little about how they are actually progressing in an assignment or how much they understood at the end of a course. The "ungrading" movement (see Blum, 2020, for a collection of essays) is gaining significant attention and holds promise for cultivating positive affect. When students are given the opportunity to participate in low-stakes (or even no-stakes) assignments, self-assessment, peer assessment, or specifications grading (see Lauricella, 2022 for ungrading practices), they can experience dramatically increased intrinsic motivation. Sharon has taught a variety of ungraded courses in which students assess themselves and their peers. In these courses, students are more willing to take risks and do something creative with their assignments rather than complete an assignment simply to get it done or prove that they know something. Ungrading is a potentially powerful avenue through which increased motivation and value contribute to students' positivity toward learning.[10]

Modeling

Instructors, too, have to walk the tightrope of positivity in one way or another. It is not just students, but also faculty, who must experience (or at least demonstrate) positive affect. "The positivity principle" argues that students are more comfortable with and learn better from instructors who demonstrate positive affect as compared to instructors who demonstrate negative affect (Lawson, 2021).[11]

Instructors can model enthusiasm for course content (Linear Algebra, hooray! Ethics is fun! Limnology will change your life!) by demonstrating their own interest in the topic, its relevance to the academic program, and its importance to students' professional future. They can also model enthusiasm for assignments, tasks, and activities by participating in them themselves (for example, joining in a game or activity), showing examples of excellent assignments that previous students have submitted, or declaring a commitment to support students' curiosity, risks, and/or ideas. An instructor with positive affect can improve student learning by increasing student motivation to engage with course content and materials to a greater degree than would instructors demonstrating negative affect.

> Even though it was an early morning class, the most fun course I had was an introductory sociology class. The instructor started the day with some kind of music playing and taught the course content with great enthusiasm, using real-world examples, facts, and discussions. Every difficult concept covered in the course was made clear for students, which made it much easier to not only learn the material, but also to realize the things we took for granted. I gained a better understanding of the how our activities and behaviors affect our daily lives.
> —A. Misra, Student, Bachelor's, Brandon University

So What? Now What?

So, you want to jump on the positivity bandwagon, put on your positivity pants, or bang the positivity drum. How? Fear not, here are some practical suggestions.

Encouraging Positive Self-Talk

"I suck at math."
"I will never understand this stupid philosophy course."

"This is so hard, but I'm going to keep at this until I get it right."
"This is not awesome, but it could totally be worse."

Most people talk to themselves or have an inner voice. Research suggests that some types of self-talk—specifically, those that are self-encouraging—are correlated with positive affect in learning situations (Oliver et al, 2010). In short, encouraging yourself such as by saying, "I can do it," is helpful. Even though many academics, this notorious group of Type-A personalities, are horribly negative in their self-talk, there is hope for them (and their students). Negative self-talk doesn't even need to be entirely replaced to have a helpful effect—it can be qualified with a positive statement. When people acknowledged a difficult situation (i.e., "this is difficult") and added a challenge statement such as, "but I can push through it" their performance was enhanced (DeWolfe, Scott & Seaman 2020). As part of encouraging positivity in the classroom, instructors can help students by encouraging them to encourage *themselves*.

Ludic Pedagogy, therefore, can help to stave off negative self-talk. By engaging students in the types of learning and learning environments in which they have a positive experience, these good learning experiences can then mitigate negative (read: self-critical) self-talk that could otherwise jeopardize meaningful learning or competence.

It's easy. Instead of allowing students to say, "I can't do this," encourage them to internalize the message "I can't do this *yet*."

Peer-to-Peer Positivity

While it is important for instructors to facilitate a positive learning environment, student-to-student interaction has a significant impact on the tone and tenor of the classroom. Students demonstrating positive extroverted behaviors such as friendliness, collaboration, willingness to communicate, and enthusiasm can elicit the same types of behaviors from peers (Eaton & Funder, 2003). The potential for peer-to-peer influence means that students and instructors have a comparable impact on the learning environment; it is not entirely up to the instructor to set and maintain the vibe in class.

It is therefore not necessary to pump positivity into the classroom through improved ventilation or by means of built-in essential oil diffusers. It is not even required to influence all students in a class equally and simultaneously. Positivity is not like a blanket. Rather, by demonstrating and maintaining positive affect and its related behaviors, one or two students can be "infected", and they will in turn assist in increasing the positive affect of their peers.[12]

For example, it is possible for a few students to ignite discussion in a classroom—we've all seen it happen. Conversation can be sparked by someone's impassioned story or response to a reading. It can take just one or two students to buy into a game, activity, or project to get others to jump on the bandwagon and participate. A mix of students is likely to happen naturally in a large group, but even in small groups, it can be helpful to organize students so that their energies are balanced. Group work can be most effective when there is a mix of extroverts (outgoing, communicative sorts) and introverts (thoughtful, quiet reflectors) in groups to achieve a balance of desirable traits and optimal group performance.

Designing Courses to Encourage Positivity
Like it or not, instructors have become (at least amateur) designers. They can adjust the colors and layout of their LMS, syllabi, handouts, and if really going all-out, open educational resources such as textbooks or resources. A study by Um et al (2011) showed that design principles in multimedia-based instructional materials can induce positive emotions. These good vibes can have a knock-off positive effect on students' learning performance, cognitive load, and other related affective experiences. Sharon is by no means a design expert, but she uses graphic design software to create her course syllabi. Rather than a typical black-and-white sea of text, she uses memes, blocks of color, and images to offset important information and eliminate walls of words. Including memes and images from popular television shows demonstrates a sense of playfulness and holds particular relevance to students. The syllabus is posted on the course LMS well before the semester begins, and thus sets the tone for a friendly learning environment before any class meetings or assignments even begin.[13]

When designing a course, it is important to build opportunities for students to experience small wins. A strategy of celebrating incremental progress toward learning goals, "small wins" will also increase the likelihood of students engaging in positive self-talk. Step-by-step progress is akin to scaffolding assignments whereby each assignment leads to the next assignment, or each assignment is a component in another, larger project. For example, many students struggle in accounting classes.[14] By helping students enjoy a sense of progress at each step of their learning as they get a grasp on the accounting equation to financial statement analysis to auditing, the overall topic no longer seems as daunting, scary, frustrating, or evocative of negative affect. If, instead, students are presented with a midterm and a final exam as the only two assessments in the same course, they are less likely to experience a sense of progress and related positive feelings. The small wins give students the opportunity to see what learning they have accomplished and to give themselves a "you got this!" pep talk when needed.

Bribe Students to Elicit Positive Affect

The use of "bribe" here is absolutely clickbait, and it really isn't the right word to use. But experimental studies of positive affect show that oftentimes positive affect must be elicited. That is, people can be prompted to feel good vibes when they are given something or perform a particular task—for example, they receive a small, unexpected gift (less than a dollar in value), watch a funny video, read humorous cartoons, or succeed in an unclear or complicated task (Ashby et al, 1999). In short, playfulness and positivity can be cultivated by means of a "reward," "treat," or "bonus."

What constitutes a playful reward? And, importantly, where can they be found on the cheap?

Creativity is the name of the game. For example, in his first meeting with a new group of students, Keith announces that he keeps a drawer full of "invisible gold stars." Students who answer questions correctly in class, show initiative, take calculated risks, or demonstrate positive behaviors, are awarded an invisible gold star. When Keith notices such a moment, he makes a big show with a gesture similar to throwing a paper airplane toward the student with a pronouncement of "Gold Star!" Absolutely nothing physical is exchanged besides laughter.

Although students sometimes look skeptical when the potential awards are explained in the first class, it is inevitable that by the end of the term some students who have not yet received an invisible gold star request one. Such requests are made in a good-humored fashion and in a joking manner (despite the hard truth of sincerely wanting one of the coveted invisible gold stars). These playful rewards are an example of inducing positive affect—and they cost nothing but a playful moment.

Conclusion

The Good Humor brand still offers its original chocolate-covered bar on a stick from the 1920s, but now boasts strawberry shortcake bars, ice-cream sandwiches, and even a Reese's bar. The feel-good, positive, playful vibe of an ice-cream treat hasn't changed, though. Positivity is like a good treat. As the affect element of Ludic Pedagogy, it allows students to experience and express the rewards of learning, enthusiasm for the course and course content, and the optimism associated with taking on the challenges of a semester, program, course, or assignment.

Most of us do not live on a diet of ice cream. It would make us feel awful and we would be broke. The same goes for positivity in class: a positive course doesn't mean a complete overhaul, for that would be inauthentic and exhausting. Positivity in higher education means a heightened awareness of the emotional aspects of learning. Students learn more and learn better when they feel good about learning. Modeling, self-talk, assessment design, and syllabus structure and presentation are all examples of how positivity can be incorporated into a course. Positivity is the mantra that *how* we teach is just as important as *what* we teach.

CHAPTER 5

Fun and Wellness

Fun, Leisure, and Learning

"What do you do for fun?" It is a question that is asked in job interviews, on dating apps, and by therapists. Responses can indicate whether a candidate is a good fit for a company, a compatible partner, or has feasible opportunities for self-care. Potential responses abound; while some might enjoy the thrill of activities such as rock climbing or travel, others enjoy games and puzzles, or arts such as music and crafts.

No matter the activity or the venue, science tells us that engaging in enjoyable activities helps with both psychological and physical functioning. For example, Pressman et al (2009) found that people who engaged in more frequent leisure activities—doing things that they enjoy—reported greater life satisfaction, lower depression, as well as lower blood pressure and better physical functioning. Similarly, Iwasaki's (2006) study showed that engaging in enjoyable activities helped the physical, psychological, social, spiritual, cultural, and altruistic aspects of stress and coping. In other words, taking part in or doing things that we enjoy not only gives us pleasure but also benefits our health in a number of ways and on a variety of levels.

Let's not mince words, though: leisure invokes the notion of fun *outside* the bounds of obligations such as work or school. And leisure and fun are not interchangeable terms. Leisure is the stuff that one chooses to do as a hobby or activity when they are not engaged in the necessities of day-to-day life, such as their job, career, or education. Fun can—and should—be had during leisure activities. However, fun can also be found in large or small parts when one is working, studying, or in otherwise challenging situations. We've all had surprise moments of fun in unexpected places—a work meeting that broke out in laughter, physical labor made enjoyable in the company of others, or study sessions in which hilarious acronyms helped with the memorization of terms or concepts.[1] These precious moments of fun can transform something from tedious to tolerable and, when we are extremely lucky, even enjoyable.

Semantics aside, a key component in the cultivation of wellness is enjoyment: if someone is enjoying an activity, no matter the context of work or play, the activity has the potential to improve both mental and emotional health. It logically follows, then, that if students *enjoy* learning, their physical and emotional health can be improved. This enjoyment—or "excitement" as bell hooks (1994) described—is a fundamental aspect of Ludic Pedagogy. In this chapter, the focus is on how Ludic Pedagogy can have a positive impact on student wellness.

What's the Status of Student Mental Health?

College and university students have long struggled with mental health issues such as exhaustion, burnout, depression, anxiety, and feeling overwhelmed. On one hand, such challenges are hallmarks of the 18 to 24 age group: at this age, post-secondary students are in the developmental stage of emerging adulthood, which Arnett (2000) argues is a period of frequent change and when "various possibilities in love, work, and worldviews are explored" (p. 469). It is no surprise that as students are on their own for the first time, managing a budget, meeting new people, and adjusting to a new learning system, they'll encounter difficulties. In addition, the traditional university system in which they will find themselves is rife with competition, grading, ranking, and testing. Constant concerns about grade point average, conflicting deadlines, exams, and other high-stakes issues do not serve to help students in an otherwise already challenging time period.

And to call out the obvious, COVID-19 may have permanently changed the nature of what it means to be a student. Much of learning has shifted online, which has demanded immediate changes, and for better or worse, online learning is here to stay. Through this necessary transformation of education, the pandemic hijacked much of student life, leaving many students lonely, unable to either meet new friends or connect with their established relationships on campus. Professional opportunities such as co-ops, experiential learning, and job placements were delayed, limited, or canceled (Wall, 2020). As a result, many students have experienced additional financial difficulties. In a 2021 survey of undergraduate students, *all* respondents reported being negatively affected by the pandemic in some way, and 59 percent reported high levels of psychological impact (Browning et al, 2021).

In the context of the significant and negative effects of the pandemic, Holmes et al (2020) declared that there exists an urgent need for research to better address how mental health concerns for vulnerable groups—university students, in particular—can be alleviated under pandemic conditions. Yet this call is not new: reports of an increase in mental health issues among post-secondary students pre-dated the COVID-19 pandemic (e.g., Kessler et al., 2005; Blanco et al., 2008; American College Health Association, 2016). Well before the coronavirus shuttered campus pubs and lecture halls, print and online media were already using terms such as "epidemic" and "crisis" (e.g., Beaudette, 2016; Chiose, 2016; Lunau, 2012) to describe the increase in concerns relative to student mental health. In 2016, university and college mental health counselors were "drowning in mental health needs" (Pfeffer, 2016), and a survey of post-secondary students showed that rates of depression, anxiety, and suicidality had all increased over a three-year period (American College Health Association, 2016). As students return to post-pandemic on-campus learning, campus counseling centers are so overwhelmed with the need for therapists and counselors that they fear they will never "be able to hire their way out" of the staffing shortage (Hernandez, 2022).[2]

It was spiritually enlightening in my final year getting to know my classmates who I had been with for four years, properly and on a more intimate level.

Sharon had us conduct an exercise where we all stood in two lines and faced each other, spoke about something personal with the person facing us for about a minute, and then moved up the line to the next person. I got to know some of my classmates on a deeper level; some of them were people with whom I had only ever just exchanged a hello with—and perhaps not even that. By the end of the exercise, I had broken the line and was hugging and crying with a girl who had basically been a stranger to me ten minutes prior to that exercise.

What stands out to me is the uniqueness of the activity. Everyone in class had different outcomes to the experiences Sharon introduced to us; however, all results were positive towards our growth. All affected us in various areas of our life. I have used some of Sharon's team-building exercises at my current workplace and my coworkers loved it.

In that final year of university, I made some amazing friends that I still have to this day. One of my best friends is a result of that class. We truly

> connected on that class trip, and although I haven't seen her in two years, we still make sure to FaceTime, call, or text each other almost daily.
> —Mahin D., Student, Bachelor's, Ontario Tech

The landscape of mental health on college and university campuses is not a pretty one, and it is arguably the only systemic change that can address this evergreen problem. The confluence of developmental changes that students experience (from doing their own laundry to relationship challenges) and educational pressures (that dreaded GPA!) demands an innovative approach to the entirety of student life, including teaching and learning. Instructors can not only alleviate some degree of stress and anxiety by implementing components of Ludic Pedagogy, but we can also work to show students that learning can be enjoyable. Inviting an enjoyable learning experience—one that incorporates fun, play, playfulness, and positivity—has the potential to benefit student health and wellness. Such an approach that addresses how it actually *feels* to learn has the potential to transform what it means to experience an optimal learning environment.

Neuroplasticity

Until recently, scientists believed that if specific areas of the adult brain were damaged, the nerve cells were unable to create new connections, and that any functions relative to this specific area of the brain would be lost. However, contemporary scholarship is in direct contrast to this now outdated view: research has shown that the brain actually *does* continue to reorganize itself and form new neural connections (Valentin, 2017). This reorganization is called "neuroplasticity," or the ability of the brain to rewire, grow, or reorganize itself. Neuroplasticity is inherent in any growth or developmental experience and is summarized by the notion that cellular and synaptic properties of the brain invoke a change in behavior (Shaw & McEachern, 2000, p. 6). Put simply, neuroplasticity is responsible for learning, behavioral change, the creation (or breaking) of habits, and even recovery from brain injuries.

Cultivating neuroplasticity is therefore, from the point of view of educators, highly desirable. There's some Ludic Pedagogy for that.

Play and Neuroplasticity

One of the most powerful ways to cultivate neuroplasticity is via play. Research has shown that playing games—and particularly digital games—improves cognitive functioning. In particular, the use of mobile games has been shown to improve cognitive performance among adults between the ages of 60 and 80 (Bonnechere et al, 2021). Similarly, digital brain training games have been shown to improve cognitive functioning, including memory and processing speed, among young adults (Nouchi et al, 2013). Even strategy games played in a traditional board game format can improve functioning in areas of the brain associated with positive experiences and enthusiasm, as well as stress reduction and a sense of calm (Jung et al, 2013).

Therefore, to grow brain cells, think more quickly, have positive vibes, reduce stress, and be calm, we should play games. The notion of playing games is particularly important because *any* kind of game—digital or analog—can help cognitive functioning and the growth of neural brain cells. Given this evidence, it is a wonder that the entire educational system isn't based on playing games!

In the absence of a complete systemic overhaul,[3] we can at least acknowledge that games have significant potential in post-secondary education, and there should be a concentrated effort to incorporate more play into the learning process. Chapter 2, "Play," addressed the *learning* benefits of games in higher education. The benefits of games can be even more significant when one considers the additional mental and physical health benefits of play and the concurrent mental health issues that are rife in the student population.

Game designer Jane McGonigal (2010) argues that playing games is the opposite of depression: when people play games, they focus their energy—often with great enthusiasm—and usually get better at a particular task, virtual situation, or game as a whole. McGonigal's focus is specifically on video games, but her argument can be easily applied to online educational games. For example, Alison Mann of the University of Toronto uses the free, web-based tool Baamboozle (www.baamboozle.com) to start class with an engaging hook, and also uses this tool to help students review course concepts before formal assessment. While not as nuanced as the online quiz tool Quizlet (www.quizlet.com), Baamboozle is based on simplicity and ease of use. If you're new to incorporating games into class, whether online or face-to-face, Baamboozle is a good place to start.

The simple and lighthearted interface of tools such as Baamboozle, Quizlet, Blooket, or Kahoot[4] implies the low-stakes and playful nature of online educational games. Most incorporate music into the preamble to the game as students log on or during the moments in which they can respond to questions. The sense of positivity and play invoked by these games can serve to put students at ease as they engage. Sharon was concerned that the simple interface of these online games could be unsuitable for higher education courses, but students appreciated the nonserious presentation of serious concepts. She asked students if the graphics and images in these sites were off-putting, but the unanimous response was that the games were fun and a welcome addition to class.

These same concepts and benefits also apply to traditional, non-technology-based play and games. There are many examples of post-secondary instructors using board games to illustrate or reinforce course concepts, but not all play needs to be game based. For example, Keith has had students play with Duplo building blocks[5] to help illuminate team development processes. In this situation, students were randomly sorted into four- or five-person teams and each team was provided with a bucket of assorted Duplo blocks. Each team was instructed to work together to build a freestanding tower out of the blocks that was taller than any other team's structure. Beginning with the word "Go!" students worked together to play with the building blocks to build their tower in any way, shape, or form they wanted. The only rule was that at the end of the building period, the tower needed to be freestanding. After the judging of tower heights, Keith led the class in a reflection of the stages of team development through which each of their teams likely had passed. The activity is just that: a fun activity. No grades, no rewards, no punishment. Nada, Zip. Just fun and learning.

Low-stakes (or no-stakes), playful activities in which students participate without experiencing punitive measures are particularly important to student mental health. Most students expect their classes to be serious or even boring (many students have been initiated by an instructor who uses PowerPoint as a teleprompter). It is liberating indeed to play a game or participate in an activity that either counts for very little—or doesn't count for marks at all.

The social nature of games is not to be underestimated. Playing group games in a work or educational setting can increase trust, bonding, a sense of connection, and a friendlier atmosphere (Petelczyk et al, 2017). Communication professor Shawna Malvini Redden of California State University at Sacramento does a "beer(less) pong" activity with her students that she found out about from Keith Chan (2014). On opposite ends of a rectangular table (or whatever shape table is present in class), Malvini Redden organizes red Solo cups in a triangle (much like how pool balls are arranged) and teams assemble on either end of the table.[6] Each cup contains a slip of paper with a question relating to the course—it could be a question to address in class, or something that students should know for an upcoming exam. From one end of the table to the other, students throw a ping-pong ball toward the opposite cups, and answer the question in which the ball lands. Rules can be made up to suit the length of time available and the purpose of the game, but the idea of using beer(less) pong and corresponding questions, while somewhat irreverent, is fun and keeps students' attention. And who can forget an answer that they learned from bouncing a ping-pong ball into a red Solo cup while not even drinking?!

Play is a natural event. Most mammals engage in play, but many avian species and even some reptiles and invertebrates have been observed in play behavior (Siviy & Panskepp, 2011). Studies examining the benefits of play among mammals have been unable to confirm that play benefits social cohesion (Sharpe, 2005) or reduces aggression (Sharpe & Cherry, 2003). However, scientists have observed that rats that played more learned more quickly, and with an increase in interactive play came more rapid brain growth (Ferchmin & Eterovic, 1982). It therefore follows that play is profoundly important for brain development, and that opportunities for play—especially in unexpected venues—ought to be welcome and celebrated.

Play and fun can be found in surprising places. During the (many) COVID-19 lockdown(s), people joked that the trash bins "went out" more than they did, so they dressed up in costume or black tie to bring the bins to the side of the road (Moschella & Radnofsky, 2020). A search on social media for the hashtag #binisolationouting shows the playful and downright funny things that people did just to take out the trash. A simple activity that invokes a playful spirit—something silly or fun—can help to lighten the mood, raise spirits, and build connections. For example, Thomas Meskill of the University of Connecticut School of Law designed Cards Against Legal Research and Cards Against Case Law games—a twist on the popular game *Cards Against Humanity* (Forbes & Thomas, 2022). Meskill created question prompts in the form of legal sentences with strategic words missing, together with a series of cards with potential answers. He demonstrated how the game worked so that anyone unfamiliar with the game would understand how to play. Meskill reports that a great deal of laughter ensues while playing this game; in student surveys at the end of the course, 92 percent of students reported that the game was "fun" or "extremely fun," and 85 percent of students said that they learned a lot from playing the game. Words that the students used to describe the game were "fun," "awesome," and "exciting."

The positive emotional aspects of fun and play are so powerful that even *thinking* about and writing down instances of playfulness experienced or observed helps enhance well-being and lowers depression scores (Proyer et al, 2021). Even if students don't want to take part in a game or silly activity, they could watch or remember it, and *still* experience some of the benefits of play.[7] Watching others in a role-play in class, observing classmates play a game, or remembering a game in which students themselves participated can all help to improve mental health. An increase in social connections, laughter, and collaboration in the context of games and play are important for this sociodemographic group.

Moving Play and Neuroplasticity
Most people struggling with mental health issues are directed to get outside, go to the gym, walk, lift weights, or simply move around more. There is a growing body of literature suggesting that exercise improves mental health by reducing anxiety and depression and can even improve the quality of life for those living with schizophrenia (Callaghan, 2004). The reasons why physical activity can help one's emotional state include effects such as reducing inflammation, increasing immunological functions, and improving the operation of biological mechanisms such as endorphins, neurotransmitters, and mitochondria (Mikkelsen, 2017). The myriad benefits of physical activity make it clear that sitting for a three-hour class period is not optimal for *anyone*, especially students—a group which is, on the whole, generally more prone to anxiety, depression, burnout, and overwhelm.

Ratey's bestselling *Spark* (2008) argues that physical activity is the single most powerful tool available to optimize brain function. It is a bold argument: exercise is *the* portal to improved cognitive wellness. Ratey claims that physical activity is the panacea for just about anything that ails us—physiological or emotional. His argument is so vehement that it would convince anyone to ditch any print version of a book in favor of the audio file so that they can listen to it while walking, running, going up stairs, or moving in any way whatsoever. In practical terms, it follows that people with sedentary jobs need to move more often (this does not come as a surprise) and need to do something that they find enjoyable, such as a sport, activity, or hobby that gets them moving. And anyone with a fitness watch knows the buzzing nudge when one has been sitting for too long.[8]

In the context of education, Ratey's argument, together with the ever-increasing body of literature suggesting that physical activity helps to mitigate a variety of ailments (for example Kraepelien, 2018; Lewis et al, 2018; Philippot, 2022) implies that physical activity ought to be incorporated into classroom activities. But let's be real, it is unlikely[9] that an Economics class will break out into a fifteen-minute basketball game once per hour, or that science classes would include purposeful walking while carrying heavy items from one lab to another for the sake of exercise. However, it *is* possible to incorporate movement into activities and to get students physically moving beyond going to the campus coffee shop during a break in class. This purposeful movement of students in the classroom is not difficult to implement and carries with it a range of positive outcomes.

For example, Sharon does an activity in her Communication Ethics course that pairs theoretical frameworks with practical concepts. The course addresses perspective: what one sees and how one sees it affects how one presents it. Fundamental characteristics such as gender, age, and ethnicity can affect one's perspective, as can specific qualities such as whether a student is in the first or fourth year or whether they commute to or live on campus. To illustrate, Sharon asks students to take a photo or video in the classroom building and post it on social media (students decide which channel; recently it has been Instagram stories or TikTok) while hashtagging the address of the building. After about fifteeen minutes, the class searches for media with the hashtag. Some students post photos of the stairwell, some post the exterior, and some post the interior. Some post videos of the study area, the café, or the classroom. The class engages in discussion about why they chose to represent the building this way, and together finds themes in the media. Perspective matters.

If you're really planning to go all out, consider taking students to an off-site program or excursion. An ambitious approach would be taking students on a weeks-long course in the form of a hiking "pilgrimage," as Kip Redick, professor and chair of the Department of Philosophy and Religion at Christopher Newport University, has been doing for decades. In these treks along the Appalachian Trail, while he and students carry tents, food, and sleeping gear, he discusses with students the notion of liminal space, hospitality, the spiritual journey, and the notion of identity. This unconventional approach gives students a practical experience with what it means to be on a journey, what it means to travel, to wait, and to transform. If your university is less inclined to be welcoming of a novel approach like Newport's, smaller-scale "trips" can be a segue into the unconventional. After seven years of petitioning her dean to let her take students away, Sharon taught an elective course on Listening—the first communication course (or any course, for that matter) at Ontario Tech that included an extended offsite, overnight trip. Over thirty students signed up for the first iteration of this new course, which was taught for four weeks face-to-face and culminated in a four-day trip to a conservation area. The trip included listening games, exercises in empathy, guided walks, and a nighttime hike to listen for owls and coyotes.

Caveats
While games can be helpful to both learning and wellness, there are caveats to ensuring the most helpful experiences in terms of emotional wellness.

Most edtech games including Blooket and Kahoot will display leaderboards at the conclusion of each question: the leaderboards indicate which students answered most quickly and scored the right answers. We've found that often students find this playful competition fun, with shouts of "YESSSSS!" or cheers for their team's correct answer.

However, leaderboards can be problematic for some groups of students, as they may fear stereotype threat (Christy & Fox, 2014). Steele and Aronson (1995) define stereotype threat as "being at risk of confirming . . . a negative stereotype about one's group." In other words, stereotype threat means that an individual fears that his or her actions or behaviors will affirm negative ideas about a social, economic, ethnic, race, or gender group to which he or she belongs. For example, undergraduate women may fear that they will confirm stereotypes about not being good at math, or students from low socioeconomic groups may be concerned that they may affirm stereotypes that they are less academically successful than other groups.

There are ways of mitigating stereotype threat in higher education. First, faculty ought to affirm students' abilities, and celebrate a growth mindset. Encouraging students to understand that success is not a fixed trait, but one that is learned and practiced, can result in greater enjoyment and engagement (Aronson, Fried, & Good, 2002). That is, when playing games, students should know that a game is low-stakes and is just practice to help them learn a new skill or concept. Second, instructors can teach students about stereotype threat; simply explaining stereotype threat can reduce its effect (Johns, Schmader, & Martens, 2005). A brief discussion about what stereotype threat is, and who may be affected, can help students potentially affected by this phenomenon to disregard its threat. Finally, students can be encouraged to use codenames when they participate in a game with a leaderboard. This way, students can be anonymous, and can be less concerned about broadcasting their performance.[10]

Positive Pedagogy

Ludic Pedagogy aims to help students learn *better* and learn *more*. When students have fun, play, are playful, and have a positive attitude, they are more comfortable, happier, and experience enhanced learning opportunities. They can remember their academic work and course concepts with more clarity than they would have if they sat passively in a one-directional classroom.

By the time students finish their undergraduate studies, they have spent at least seventeen years in an educational setting. In early education, parents expect that schools will provide their children with the necessary skills, safety, and knowledge appropriate for their age. In higher education, students pay for—and expect that—they will receive the training required for a career. But post-secondary institutions have become increasingly responsible for emergency healthcare, social activities, food, and safety. So, what is the true responsibility of an academic institution? Is it simply to provide an academic education, or is it to supply support for students in all the other ways?

The positive pedagogy movement (Seligman & Adler, 2018) suggests that student well-being is fundamental to education. Positive pedagogy means that students are affected not only by *what* is taught, but also *how* a teacher educates (for review, see Shankland & Rossett, 2017). The philosophy argues that skills for happiness should be taught in schools, but also that the way such skills are taught is fundamental to how students respond and process their own sense of well-being (Waters, 2021). Elements of wellness such as goal setting, play, and mindfulness can be weaved into lessons about any subject or in any context, such as math, fine arts, science, business, or languages. Positive pedagogy suggests that wellness can be inherent in all subjects and levels of education by using examples, stories, or a background that suggests that well-being is fundamental to one's daily life.

However, positive pedagogy has been examined almost exclusively in the K–12 system; proponents of this philosophy have not yet considered to any great degree whether the principles in primary and secondary education are applicable to higher education. The dearth of research on positive pedagogy in the post-secondary arena may be simply because this pedagogical development is new. It may also be because many universities tend to place significant value on research over teaching, thus limiting resources allocated to the development and analysis of this teaching philosophy. Yet positive pedagogy would find a welcome home in post-secondary education given the needs of undergraduate students and the myriad issues facing university and college students.

Ludic Pedagogy does not propose that faculty need explicitly or implicitly teach students about wellness.[11] However, fun, play, playfulness, and positivity have direct and evidence-based links to positive mental health, social cohesion, a sense of belonging, and overall well-being. To that end, positive pedagogy and Ludic Pedagogy are compatible educational philosophies whereby the well-being of students is fundamental to their academic and personal success. While Ludic Pedagogy does not directly attempt to teach students about wellness, it is by nature an avenue toward well-being. Each of the elements of Ludic Pedagogy is known to lead to improved academic success and emotional stability, thus creating a space for students to create social networks, emotional connections, and learning communities—all hallmarks of a successful higher education experience.

Fun as Scholarly Stress Management

It's no wonder that R&B/pop musician Usher's line, "Sleeping is forbidden at the age of 22. It's all work and no play," is so memorable. Student life usually includes projects, studying for exams, writing papers, managing scholarships and funding, planning internships or work experience, and finding time to do laundry (maybe). A large percentage of students have jobs—part or full time—during the school year. If students are managing family responsibilities—caring for children, siblings, or parents—the demands are even greater. In the 2020s, add a pandemic, and simple survival is a legitimate daily concern; even keeping up to date with vaccines and public health requirements has become a new level of responsibility.

The "work hard, play hard" mentality has long been a university trope. Consider John Belushi's character John "Bluto" Blutarsky in *Animal House*. He dons the ubiquitous COLLEGE sweater and represents college students at parties everywhere. Ludic Pedagogy is not meant to be used as a justification for or an endorsement of "Anything But A Cup" parties or Thirsty Thursday pub nights,[12] but it *does* promote fitting more fun and play into students' days in wholesome ways.

On the macro level, the whole of student life invokes big problems and, therefore, big parties. The whole system cannot be overhauled in one fell swoop. Suggesting "have more fun" as a remedy for what ails students is unlikely to get traction. However, on the micro-level, faculty can change each individual course to be more fun and playful. In each individual class meeting, instructors can help students to associate learning with enjoyment. With each topic addressed, we can support a playful—that is, curious and inquisitive—attitude so that students can approach challenging topics with a sense of inquiry and interest.

A walk across campus or a look at university meme pages shows that university life can be demanding, exhausting, expensive, stressful, or any combination of such wearying qualities in differing quantities throughout the term. And it is abundantly clear that meltdowns, tears, and sleepless nights all appear to be requisite to the post-secondary experience, or at least they're made to seem like an essential feature of the exam period. Yet, fun can negate fear. If the topic or activity is fun, it becomes less daunting. For example, an English major would certainly quake in their boots over the thought of a final exam in physics. Enter Chris Whittaker, who teaches physics for non-majors at Dawson College in Montreal. He scheduled a creative—but challenging—final exam. Rather than a traditional pencil and paper test, he reserved a movie theater during the exam period and took the class to see *Doctor Strange in the Multiverse of Madness*. He asked students to report to him what they understood the filmmakers got right or wrong about physics in the film.[13]

Before an exam, presentation, speech, or other academic performance, students are likely to feel nervous, have racing thoughts, or a pounding heart. All such sensations are normal.[14] The perception of these sensations, however, is what can make the difference between discomfort and overwhelm versus anticipation and excitement. When a student feels problematic sensations such as anguish or significant upset, they are experiencing *distress*. However, when students experience a sense of nervousness associated with expectation, possibility, or intention, they are experiencing *eustress*. Eustress contributes to well-being and is considered beneficial to one's development. This "positive" stress can lead to feelings of optimism and a positive outlook on life (Aschbacher et al, 2013). The goal of instructors is to help students to feel capable, motivated, interested, and positively engaged, thus maximizing eustress and minimizing distress. When students feel capable of taking on a challenge, they become more motivated, interested, and positively engaged—all of which are key emotional states and correspond with overall well-being and life satisfaction (McGonigal, 2010).

Nowhere in the Ludic Pedagogy model is the suggestion made that students experience a stress-free, simplified, good-vibes-only university life. A watered-down academic experience would not prepare anyone for professional work or (gasp!) graduate school. Rather, the model argues that when stress is present, students ought to be given the tools to be able to transition from distress to eustress. Once students feel as if they are prepared for an exam, presentation, or other academic experience, they can take on the next one with increased confidence.

Looking toward Wellness

Ludic Pedagogy is not meant to be a tool for eliminating all stress from the lives of post-secondary students. Higher education is, by almost any definition, a stressor which is itself compounded by the everyday stressors of day-to-day functioning and, currently, with those of a (hopefully waning) pandemic.

In terms of student wellness, what this model does hope to achieve is twofold. First, Ludic Pedagogy aims to highlight that *how* we teach impacts students as much, if not more, than *what* is taught. The methods by which instructors present material to their students and assess how well they have learned that material has a direct impact on their well-being. The second aim of the model is to not diminish the stress students feel—it is, as has been noted, part and parcel of higher education—but, instead, to reorient that stress. Instead of a harmful, destructive form of stress, Ludic Pedagogy aims to reorient it into a positive, growth-oriented form of stress.

The mental health of university students is already in a dangerous place. While we should not diminish the integrity of our courses, we can certainly change the way things are done. By implementing the ideals of fun, play, playfulness, and positivity, we as instructors can do our part to make higher education the positive, transformational experience it should be.

CHAPTER 6

Implementation and Impacts

So you, an academic, want to have more fun.

Your students—undergrads, graduates, even PhDs—want to have more fun.

The Ludic Pedagogy model proposes three patented[1] questions to consider guiding Ludic Pedagogy principles. If you are confident in having fun, start here. If you have no idea of what you're doing, start here. With every course, assignment, activity, or academic interaction, start here:

1. Will this [reading, activity, assignment, conversation, lab] make my students more interesting at parties?
2. Would I want to do this activity or assignment?
3. Will I find happiness in my life when I am grading or giving feedback on this activity or assignment?

The answers to all three questions should be a resounding "YES!"

These questions are helpful as you're designing your syllabus, populating your LMS, and getting to know your students as the semester continues. Start here, continue here, and end here.

1. The Party Test

Before assigning any course material including (but not limited to) readings, assignments, class activities, or projects, legitimately ask yourself, "Will this make my students more interesting at parties?"

This question doesn't refer to the student's ability to answer Jeopardy or Trivial Pursuit questions; it's not about the recall of facts or formulas.[2] Rather, it considers whether a student understands the content well enough that they can pull out the most pertinent aspects and clearly explain it to their grandmother, their crush, or a total stranger. Albert Einstein said that physical theories "ought to lend themselves to so simple a description 'that even a child could understand them'" (Clark, 1972).

In other words, students should be able to understand what they have learned well enough that they can explain it to someone at a party.

There are two key components to consider when deciding if any course content or assessment passes the party test. Both answers must be in the positive in order for the material to find a home on the syllabus. If not, it ends up in the circular file.[3]

First issue: is the reading/lesson/assignment/whatever helpful, illustrative, and actually, really, truly important? Now stop rolling your eyes and exclaiming with great indignation, "Yes! Everything I teach is absolutely essential!" Take objective stock of the downright necessity of your course content and you may find outdated examples, references to popular culture with which students aren't familiar, or anything that is past its due date.

In the throes of pandemic teaching, many of us took a long, hard look at our courses—determining the most important concepts or readings, what open-access readings could replace expensive textbooks, and which assignments could be reduced, reused, or recycled. Fortunately, we don't need a pandemic every year or two to do this work. Every year, pandemic or not, you have an opportunity to replace anything stale with new or contemporary work. In other words, ditch the busywork, include new scholarship along with the classics, and replace your pop culture examples that are contemporary enough for students to "get" them. If you're not sure what's cool on social media, TikTok is a great place to go down the rabbit hole to try to find out what is going on.

Second issue: does the topic/lesson/assignment give students the opportunity to express their understanding? Traditionally, in higher education, faculty assign an exam or an essay. Instead consider a method by which students can tell a story about this concept, apply it in the context of their own lives, or put it in their own words. Have they interacted with the material deeply enough that they will remember the case study they debated, or when a similar situation emerges, will they have sufficient experience with it to explain what they discovered or discussed in class? Students should have enough of an understanding so that they discuss it even when their heart is pounding in the company of someone they find tremendously attractive. There's the final exam in situ.

"Not all students go to parties," some may protest. Or, "I have a class of introverts!" Both arguments are non-starters. Students don't need to be extroverts to be interesting at parties. Introverts are reflective, thoughtful people. They are interesting by definition. Further, the definition of "party" as it is used here is very liberal: it could be a family gathering, online game night, work event, or a one-on-one coffee date. A party is not limited to Bridgerton-quality dress and live music, nor is liquid smoke requisite. Students participate in Discord groups, video game communities, and online meetups. Parties consist of any number of people, in both the virtual and analog world, in a near-infinite number of contexts.

Consider a simple example of applying the party test. A student is traveling with some friends and they go to an art museum. A history course would be handy in this context for sure. But political science students could explain the socioeconomic conditions resulting in the representation of subjects. Communication students might consider the promotional material for the museum, look for virtue signaling in art, or imagine who was or is the audience for specific pieces. Economics or business students are sure to ponder the cost of entry or why some pieces are more financially valuable than others. Engineers could take note of the flow of people throughout the museum or structure in art, and science students could explain why and how some pieces of art are climate controlled. There's a place for everyone in this party of life.

There is no shortage of fertile ground for the party test. For example, Sharon teaches a first-year Public Speaking class. Given that many people fear speaking in front of a group more than they fear death, this course is a prime venue for training in being interesting (or at least comfortable) at parties. But that doesn't ensure that the materials pass the party test. The content that Sharon includes in the precious twelve weeks of the course could make or break it. She teaches students to breathe through anxiety, how to pose a thoughtful question of a colleague, and ways to analyze their audience. Does she need to include a unit on business communication? Probably not, because there's a whole course on that in the following year. Assuming that interesting people attend parties with other interesting people,[4] students can talk about their course of study or a particular concept anywhere, but they need to be able to have sufficient mastery of course content to do so. And as people who teach, well, that's literally our job.

Giving students the opportunity to practice extemporaneous use of course content is a great way to pass the party test. Keith teaches a course on negotiation—a key skill in human communication and business. Further to readings and theoretical instruction, he organizes role-play activities to illustrate and practice negotiation concepts. Role-play scenes are a great way to practice the practical context of theoretical and academic information. One of his (and students') favorite role-play activities is when teams of students negotiate the purchase and sale of an intergalactic spaceship. Both the topic and the method of this activity pass the party test: negotiation is a great skill to have, and an intergalactic spaceship isn't something anyone comes across in any old undergraduate course. While engaging in this fun classroom activity, students get creative with the benefits of a spaceship, and the laughter is a bonus. Students can be interesting at parties by talking about the course content *or* the activity itself.

Most assignments that students complete will not help make them interesting at parties. The same tired essay prompts, lab experiments, and exams are not going to spark up a conversation, unless of course it's to complain about them. What's more is that these kinds of assignments, once completed, are only ever seen by the student and the instructor or teaching assistant. Then, they are deleted from one's files, thrown away (or maybe, if they are lucky, recycled in the blue bin), or archived by the course LMS. Assignments that pass the party test are not going to end up sad, lonely, and tossed aside like a bag of moldy tangerines.

Instead, assignments that pass the party test invite students to be *producers* rather than passive *consumers* of information. In Sharon's third-year Ethics course, she introduces students to a variety of blogging sites (the site of choice will change with new emergent technologies). Throughout the course, students post eight times; at the end of the term, they have a full-on blog portfolio that can be shared with potential employers (or partygoers, as the case may be). Given that 90 percent of potential employers check candidates' social media profiles, it's not a bad idea for students to have some posts—or even a dedicated account—relative to their academic course of study. A post about what a lab experiment means for the local lake or how a legal issue manifests in a contemporary case can make an illustrative social media post while still allowing the student to remain "on brand."

2. The Self-Reflexive Desire and Interest Question

Put simply, before presenting students with a fun, silly, or new activity, making them do an academic/online/paid for or free reading, consider this:

Would I want to do this activity/reading/project/lab/assignment/test/fill-in-the-blank-here?

Seriously, would you? Is the assignment (or exam or whatever) you are giving to your students something that you would be interested in doing? Don't try to cast yourself back into the role of a student—think about your current preferences and inclinations. If you were told that you had to do every one of your assignments alongside your students, how would you feel?

Excited? Defeated? Passionate? Bored? It is very likely that your students feel much the same as you do.

There is a very easy test to answer this question and to ensure that your answer is honest. Channel your inner athlete and "just do it."

When assigning something to students—a research paper, a set of problems, an audio-visual presentation, whatever—do the assignment with them. Not only will you get a firsthand understanding of how students may feel when doing the assignment, but you may also identify ways in which future iterations of the assignment may be improved.[5] Maybe the time frame you have allotted to the students to do the assignment is too short or too long. Maybe the scope of the assignment is too broad or too narrow. Maybe the resources you are asking the students to use are not readily available. Maybe the assignment just . . . *sucks*. Or maybe it is way more fun than you thought, and you get a good idea for a forthcoming paper, entry into a pedagogy journal, or blog post.

Correlated to enjoyment is the level of "disposability" of an assignment or coursework.

Most work that students do is simply disposable: once the work has completed its duty as an assessment tool, it winds up in the recycling bin or the celebratory end-of-year bonfire. And while this may be considered the way of things, consider the amount of wasted effort put into a product that serves such a limited function. Students, too, may do this mental calculus and decide to only put in "just enough" effort on such an activity. It is very possible that the quality of work that students would provide for *non-disposable* assignments could be significantly greater. Academics don't write work and then throw it away—why should students?

Non-disposable assignments are those that continue to have a life and purpose beyond that of a lowly course assessment. Also called "open pedagogies" or "renewable assignments" this kind of work has an audience beyond the faculty member or any marking assistants (Wiley, 2013). This means that the assignment could be applied research for a particular entity, such as an organization, charity, or business. It could be something like a student-organized publication, social media account, website blog, outreach activity, podcast, or poster (for examples, see Jhangiani and DeRosa, n.d.). Non-disposable assignments could be submitted in the form of a social media post, a website, a podcast, a piece of art, or a collaborative online textbook created as part of the course (for descriptions and outlines, see Wiley, 2013).

Simply knowing that people beyond the instructor will see their work— that it has a purpose beyond that of an assessment tool—will help to get the best out of students. Further, it will provide them with a concrete example of their work that can assist in establishing and growing their professional lives. In other words, the assignment is relevant to the student's learning, to the community, or to their future in a clear and meaningful way. The assignment can still involve research, group work, and be graded, but relevance is fundamental. Research shows that students like these kinds of assignments better, see the value in them, and are more motivated to work on them (Sheu & Grissett, 2022).

> In a Local Politics course during my undergrad, I was encouraged to go into a Winnipeg neighborhood to learn about grassroots movements going on there. I was exposed to a co-op of women who were making and selling star blankets online, at a time when there weren't a lot of online shops.
>
> I learned about the transformative and tenuous power of co-ops, social issues faced by this group of women and, most importantly, I got out of the classroom. As a result of that class, I pursued a master's degree in City Planning and have worked in community development ever since.
> —Leanne, Student, Bachelor's, University of Winnipeg

3. Will I find happiness in my life while I am grading or giving feedback?

Okay, the original question here was, "Will I hate my life when I am grading or giving feedback," but that was a bit harsh and didn't merit a positive response, so it was recast. The goal is to invoke a resounding YES to the fundamental and patented Ludic Pedagogy questions.

In truth, we are all familiar with the inevitable end-of-semester conversation among faculty at any university or college. It happens online, face-to-face, on Twitter, and at the water cooler:

"How's your marking going?"
"Ugh! Don't ask . . . it never ends!"

Why do we choose (truly, we choose!) to design courses in ways we believe will be interesting or valuable to students[6] but then assess their learning in ways that make our *own* lives miserable? Wouldn't it make more sense to design assessments that are not only valuable to students, but also do not unnecessarily increase our own workload, misery, and stress levels?

In a perfect academic world, assessments would be designed such that they are not soul-crushing for students and still demonstrate knowledge of learning objectives. The same assessments would not feel overwhelming for instructors when we sit down to mark them. It would be great if everyone had small classes and loads of time to give students tons of feedback, support, and offer rewrites, resubmits, and endless revisions. But that is usually limited to Hogwart's School of Witchcraft and Wizardry, because they've got a fabulous endowment and as many TAs as they desire.

Witchcraft and wizardry aside, there are many ways to make assessments fun for both students and instructors—it just requires some playfulness and positivity. Educational technology (edtech, also searchable on Twitter as #edtech) can help achieve this level of fun and engagement. The landscape of edtech is constantly changing, but multimedia is a great way to get students involved with both course content and one another. For example, students can use a video recording and sharing app such as Flipgrid for low-stakes assignments: lab instructions, introductions, explanations, or even brief speeches. Flipgrid even has built-in rubrics so that grading effort is minimal (Thompson, 2022)! Persuall, a social e-reading tool, holds remarkable promise for both engaging students with one another while addressing course readings, but also alleviating grading issues on the part of the instructor. Perusall's built-in algorithms can be adjusted to the instructor's specifications so that students' participation can be assessed automatically. All questions, comments, and responses that students make, together with time spent on readings can be incorporated into a grading scheme. Student engagement and participation can be quantified automatically. In short, some grading can be totally eliminated by using technology like Perusall.

End-of-term grading can feel like a dumpster fire. But it doesn't need to. The practice of "ungrading" rejects the idea that grades are a "gotcha" strategy so that instructors can catch and punish students for not getting it right (Lauricella, 2022). Ungrading means that educators can take into account how students demonstrate how and what they have learned in a framework that is fair and equitable. This kind of assessment strategy requires a lot of reflection on the part of both students and faculty but doing so can be rewarding because instructors get a true glimpse into what and how students are learning (Stommel, 2020). While ungrading can include specifications grading, labor-based grading, peer assessment, self-assessment, and instructor/student conferences, it means that students have the opportunity to take ownership of and agency over their own learning.

One of the most meaningful ways of developing assessments free of hate is not only about how instructors review students' work, but in what they invite students to submit. One of the most enjoyable ways to buck the assessment trend is to give students a great deal of freedom in how they present what they learn. The "unessay" is a summative assignment in which students can create a final submission in whatever format they choose. This invitation is situated in the literature on authentic assessment (Svinicki, 2004) which describes how assessments are directly relevant to student goals, professional environment, and students' personal talents and strengths. An unessay breaks away from a typical essay, research paper, or lab report.

Jones (2017) popularized the term "unessay" in a Twitter thread. When teaching his history courses, he invited students to submit final projects in creative ways. The thread is inspiring and worth the visit down the rabbit hole—students submitted needlework, paintings, stories, poetry, and stories. Similarly, Denial (2019) invites students to submit a final unessay project of their choice rather than a paper but asks students to accompany the project with a three-page reflection on what they learned from doing the project, together with a bibliography of the sources consulted and that are relevant to the course readings. For step-by-step instructions on how to try an unessay particularly in online environments, see Lauricella (2022). You're likely to actually look forward to student projects at the end of term rather than dread them.

But None of This Will Work for My Courses!

Trying to provide a recipe that will work for every course in every faculty in every institution is a non-starter. There is just no way to do it. And Ludic Pedagogy isn't meant to be a recipe—it is simply the ingredients. Just take those ingredients to create the recipe that works for you, your students, and your course content.

In other words, just try something. Anything.

And it might fail.[7] So what? Failing and rolling with it not only models for your students how to deal with failure, but a failed attempt provides a place from which to start. Think about the activity or game or joke or whatever it was, and ask the following questions:

1. What worked?
2. What could have worked better?
3. If another instructor had developed this activity, what would you suggest to them?
4. How could this activity be improved?
5. What are three specific things you can do to improve it?
6. What will you do again?
7. What will you not do again?

8. If you were a student, what would you think of the activity? What would you think of the results of the activity?
9. With what aspects of the activity were you comfortable? Least comfortable? Why?
10. Is there another way to approach this activity?
11. Are there elements of the activity to which you need to pay more attention?
12. What one change could make the biggest difference in this activity?
13. What insights did you gain from trying this activity?
14. If you saw someone else try this activity and fail, what suggestions would you make?
15. What do you do next?

Using these questions (or any other that works) to reflect on any element of your course—whether you have tried to redesign it to follow ludic principles or not—is a great place to start. You can start to identify strong points, weaknesses, and places where there is space for play, and develop ideas of where to take your students the next time through the course.

Developing fun, playful activities is hard work. These things don't just suddenly appear fully formed; they develop through successive iterations as we work to find the sweet spot. Every time you try something, you're working to make it better for the students and for yourself.

Even if something fails horribly, it can work: Be willing to laugh and admit to your students that the activity failed. Then, explain what you expected to happen, what the purpose was, or how you had envisioned the outcome would be. Debriefing students on the activity, and whether it worked or not, can be playful and positive. It acts as a valuable learning experience.

Whether your attempts at implementing Ludic Pedagogy are raging successes or dumpster-fire disasters, keep trying and reflecting. It won't take long to find that you have developed a stable full of tools that work for you and your courses—and are enjoyed by your students.

Back to the Big Picture

Implementing Ludic Pedagogy goes beyond just assessment design. It goes beyond course design. It goes to the core of our mission as teachers—helping students learn. Such a mission may sound simple, but teaching and learning in colleges and universities can feel increasingly difficult with every passing year.

The challenges facing higher education are many and varied. A report prepared for the UNESCO 2009 World Conference on Higher Education noted that "larger and more diverse student populations, a growing interest in professional education and lifelong learning, the privatization of higher education, financial constraints, enhanced attention to quality and accountability, and evolving tendencies for post-secondary institutions and national systems to situate themselves in international and global contexts are just a few of the most important trends of the last decade" (Altbach et al, 2009, p. 111).

Further, there has been a much broader acknowledgment than perhaps any other time about the problems and issues inherent in higher education. Across the board, there are many talented individuals working to improve higher education around the world in terms of accessibility, inclusiveness, decolonization, student mental health, and a wealth of other concerns that are not new but are being newly challenged.

Picture yourself preparing for a new academic year. Not only are you writing or revising the syllabi for your courses, but you also have to attend department and faculty meetings, complete the textbook requisition forms for the bookstore, deal with the regular deluge of emails, keep on top of your writing obligations, submit the journal article reviews you've been granted two extensions on already, gather the information you said you'd have ready for the next committee meeting, deal with the pile of papers on the corner of your desk from last year, find time to go to that other committee meeting (no, not that one, the *other* other one), get familiar with the accommodation requests from the new crop of students, transpose the information from last year's forms onto the new forms, and where did you put your glasses anyway? Oh, and don't forget about the budget issues, staffing requests, student recruitment activities, grant applications, funding opportunities, grad student supervision duties, faculty presentations, grade appeals, and research opportunities that need your input. By end of the day, if possible.[8]

Considered on the whole, post-secondary instructors find themselves either directly facing or operating in the context of a burdensome quantity of issues. Such an environment highlights the need for systemic change in higher education. The amount and degree of change that is required can feel overwhelming, but we suggest that Ludic Pedagogy is a useful tool for this work.[9]

The COVID-19 pandemic initiated changes in higher education that may not have otherwise happened so quickly. Course delivery, characteristics of the student body, and visions for the future have all shifted significantly. Global competition for students is fierce. The desire to attract international students has led universities and colleges to focus on developing high-impact teaching and learning strategies across the institution. A result of so many changes is the development of policies and professionals highlighting and enforcing the scholarship of teaching and learning. Individual instructors, departments, and entire institutions are focusing more on student needs assessment, inclusive learning approaches, and universal design considerations (Altbach et al, 2009).

Ludic Pedagogy is all about student engagement, retention, and improvement of education and well-being. Not only does research show that students will learn more, retain more, have a deeper understanding of course content, form better prosocial bonds, and all the other wonderful outcomes that have been identified throughout this book, but it is also likely that students will find greater joy in their education. And while positive emotions and experiences cannot solve student retention issues by themselves, they certainly can help for a significant proportion of the students lost to either not feeling the vibe or feeling abandoned in an unfamiliar world.

Those who enter higher education looking for something they struggle to define will likely not find it as an anonymous student lost in a lecture hall. Connections via Ludic Pedagogy may help students find that elusive "thing" they seek. In many cases, this thing is a sense of community—finding people of a like mind, with shared interests, values, and outlooks. Through the connections we help foster in our classroom activities, we can help students find meaningful learning communities.

Despite rising financial costs, higher education is no longer just for elites; more than ever, first-generation students are enrolling in colleges and universities. This population has lower retention rates than other groups of students (Pratt et al, 2019) due to the issues that arise from operating in a wholly unfamiliar setting. First-generation post-secondary students also want to make career decisions based on enjoying their work, not solely based on financial considerations (Gibbons & Woodside, 2012). Spending any time in an educational setting in which there is little enjoyment in the classroom is not an auspicious beginning to such career aspirations and perhaps compounds retention issues.

If enjoyment is of importance to students, then bringing enjoyment into the classroom becomes valuable on many fronts. By showing students that fun and enjoyment is present in course content, the implication is that enjoyment may also be found in the eventual workplace. Students struggling to find fulfillment in their academic work may not be able to envision a career in the field that provides the type of fulfillment that they seek.

The tools and ideas throughout this book are not incompatible with the other important work and ideas faculty need to consider for their classrooms—universal design for learning, decolonization, equity, diversity, and inclusion—all of which are very important things to consider. Ludic Pedagogy can—and, in fact, *should*—work with these initiatives to make learning more enjoyable and impactful for all. There is a wide range of institutional, social, political, and global drivers for the changes needed in higher education. Therefore, as we attempt to implement change, everything involved in education—students, faculty, classrooms, organization, and the greater context—needs to be considered (Ipek & Karaman, 2020).

Ludic Pedagogy provides a toolbox that every instructor can adapt to their individual personalities, areas of expertise, students, and teaching environments. The philosophy and tools that make up Ludic Pedagogy allow any instructor to continue an exploration toward answering the question: "What could education be?"

Conclusion

The Great Resignation—if not a direct consequence of the COVID-19 pandemic, then certainly hastened by it—has shone a bright light on what people value and desire in their working lives.[1] While much of the discussion on this economic trend of voluntary job exits has focused on employee dissatisfaction with compensation, a study by Sull, Sull & Zweig (2022) revealed that corporate culture was the most significant predictor of employees leaving an organization. It appears that people are willing to walk away from a paycheck when the environment in which that paycheck is earned creates an intolerable level of discomfort.

The perennial post-secondary issue of student retention is strikingly similar to the Great Resignation. Higher education loses students for the same reasons that industry loses employees: When the extrinsic rewards no longer outweigh the intrinsic motivation to be elsewhere, we lose *people*—whether they are employees or students.

Compensation is the extrinsic reward for employees; for students, the reward may be a diploma or the promise of their dream job. If this external force is the primary reason for a student to be in higher education, and if there is very little intrinsic motivation to learn, that student is going to be lost. A true desire to learn has to come from within: there needs to be something inside the individual that drives them forward in their education. Without that desire, we will lose the student—either their attention, their participation, or even their enrolment.

The primary intrinsic motivator to learning in Ludic Pedagogy is an element of *fun*. Together with play, playfulness, and positivity, an improved teaching and learning experience can take shape. Each of the pillars of Ludic Pedagogy is connected to and intertwined; the attributes of each element support and enhance the others. In other words, introducing one aspect of this model into the learning experience is very likely to allow or encourage others to emerge. Which tools an instructor chooses to use will be based on their personality and preferences; there is no singular method or step-by-step plan for introducing Ludic Pedagogy into one's own teaching. One only needs to be authentic in his or her attempts and have the willingness to enjoy what he or she does.

To that end, Ludic Pedagogy is not a recipe—it is only a list of the ingredients.

In practical terms, everyone implementing this model is creating their own method of ludic pedagogy. The Very Important and capitalized Ludic Pedagogy refers only to the model. The ludic elements that you introduce into your classrooms and to your students through humor, game-based learning, or general playfulness is *all you*. You can use the ingredients listed and described throughout this book to create your own bake-off.[2]

No one (including the authors) should be so naïve as to believe that adopting Ludic Pedagogy is a panacea. Teaching is hard work. There will be frustrations and there will be bad days. However, we all make choices. We can focus on the difficult or the negative. Sometimes, we enter the classroom with the goal of just getting through the day (we've all been there). Yet still, we can put in the work to create an environment that we enjoy and find fun.[3] And if we, as faculty, are having fun in the classroom, our students will enjoy themselves more than they would otherwise for no other reason than simple emotional well-being.

Models of teaching have evolved from the idea that students' failure to learn was due to their own ineptitude to a more contemporary belief that students need to be actively engaged in the learning process (Altbach et al, 2009). Teaching has become increasingly student-centered; it is focused more on the students' learning than the teacher's actions. Ludic Pedagogy is about creating a learning environment that encourages actions, attitudes, and affect that best foster the kind of student engagement that leads to deep learning.

As you have stepped through the elements of the Ludic Pedagogy model, it is likely that myriad tantalizing doors have opened through which you were provided only a brief look rather than an in-depth tour. There are dozens, if not hundreds, of useful and illustrative papers, articles, books, and blogs covering the topics this book simply did not have the space to cover. Some resources are included in the Appendix to this book, but you are encouraged to continue to discover more about those aspects of Ludic Pedagogy that best fit *your* comfort level, personality, courses, institution, and students. The best first step is to think about what is possible with (1) what you have and (2) where you are right now. Then, you can have open and honest conversations with not only your students but also colleagues at your institution and beyond.

The primary issue associated with this model is positive outcomes for students. But there is an important point that must be kept front of mind by any practitioner: the ability to engage in ludic activity, and to maintain a ludic mindset, is very much a privileged practice. Play and playful approaches to education—at any level—are not equally accessible to everyone. In order to engage in any form of ludic pedagogy, one must be privileged with the ability, time, space, confidence, inclination, and social supports to do so:

> Play has the potential to be a powerful tool for supporting learning and making the world a better place, but it is crucial to recognise the implicit power structures and exclusivity of play, and work hard to make playful learning something that is an option for all. (Whitton, 2018)

The benefits of introducing ludic elements into the classroom therefore extend well beyond benefits to learning. Such a pedagogy, properly done, both requires and provides the freedom to play, be playful, and the opportunity to have fun for those who may not normally have access to such freedoms. As instructors,[4] we need to make every effort so that our students feel safe in the learning environment.

When a learning place (whether physical or digital) becomes playful, it can help us "produce playful, creative graduates who can apply the same creative approach to their future careers as we enable in their learning" (Walsh, 2015, p. 90). Students who experience a safe and playful learning environment are poised to overcome challenges and engage with creative solutions rather than following limited, structured paths. In other words, safe and playful learning environments can prime students to think creatively and with freedom so that they can establish these thinking patterns—even when environments are less welcoming or positive.

Instructors taking on a ludic mindset, and encouraging the same in students, are perhaps training an entire generation of a workforce to enter their professions with a creative, playful, and fun mindset. With this, academics can ask, "what hath we wrought?"

The Ludic Pedagogy model is not the first musing on what kinds of awesomeness could happen if more people adopted and promoted a ludic mindset. There exists a concept called "ludic ontology." Sadly, it's a poorly defined and vague idea that play is something beyond definition or understanding, and, well, that's kind of it. Many academics will find it a breathless, navel-gazing idea that requires a lot of googling of words that are hard to spell.

On the other hand, "ludic mindset" is the idea of approaching life in the day-to-day through the lens of the four elements of the Ludic Pedagogy model. By addressing motivation, activity, affect, and attitude, a more general application of this model offers to bring educational benefits into our broader experience—that is, even outside the academy. Admittedly, this idea may seem a little breathless itself, but try with us to imagine a world in which everyone's default interaction with others in the workplace is one of fun.

Students who learned a ludic mindset throughout their education, and then enter the workforce may, over time, transform the workplace and the culture of work into a more engaging, enjoyable experience. With enough employees (and managers) having this mindset, we may see the intrinsic motivation that was fostered in educational contexts begin to emerge in the working world. There are enough toxic environments in the workplace to have triggered the Great Resignation (Sull, Sull, & Zweig, 2021), so it is time to envision a world where people *want* to go to work.

By being champions of a ludic pedagogy, you are championing a way of approaching challenging tasks in a manner that is positive, hopeful, and engaging. Students adopting this orientation as they move out of their post-secondary studies can (and hopefully, will) take this positive, playful approach out into the world, and spread it further.

The higher education experience needs more fun and play—this argument has been firmly established here in this book. So, what next? What good does it do to introduce more fun into the college and university classroom, when there is far too little of it after graduation? We have just kicked the can a little further down the road. Instead, by encouraging the adoption of a ludic mindset, we can help bring a little more light and a little more fun into the world.

The tools of Ludic Pedagogy are now in your hands. They are yours to use as you will.

Tag. You're it.

Appendix

Suggested Readings and Other Cool Stuff

Barkley, E. F. (2010). *Student Engagement Techniques: A Handbook for College Faculty.* Jossey-Bass.

Bruff, D. (2019). *Intentional Tech: Principles to Guide the Use of Educational Technology in College Teaching.* West Virginia University Press.

Darby, F. & Lang, J.M. (2019). *Small Teaching Online: Applying Learning Science in Online Classes.* Jossey-Bass.

Forbes, L. & Thomas, D. (Eds.). (2022). The PlayBook: Professors at Play. ETC Press. https://press.etc.cmu.edu/books/professors-play-playbook

Gannon, K. (2020). *Radical Hope.* West Virginia University Press.

James, A. & Nerantzi, C. (Eds.). (2019). *The Power of Play in Higher Education: Creativity in Tertiary Learning.* Palgrave Macmillan.

Kay, R. & Hunter, W.J. (Eds.). (2022). *Thriving Online: A Guide for Busy Educators.* Ontario Tech University.

The Ludicast—the Ludic Pedagogy podcast—available wherever you get your podcasts, with all episodes archived at www.LudicPedagogyLab.com

Lang, J. M. (2016). *Small Teaching: Everyday Lessons From the Science of Learning.* Jossey-Bass.

Norgard, R., Solheim, J., & Bukholt, K.J. (Eds.). (2021). *Playful Higher Education: Voices, Activities & Co-creations from the PUP Community.* Center for Higher Education Futures, Danish School of Education, Aarhus University.

Examples of non-disposable assignments: http://openpedagogy.org/category/assignment/ and https://open.uaf.edu/non-disposable-assignments-and-why-you-should-use-them/

Online Resources for Making and Customizing Games

Blooket: An online game for review materials. The free version allows some game modes and the paid version allows some more creative features. There are many possibilities including players stealing points, trading points, collecting virtual candy, traveling a racetrack, going to the supermarket, and more. Blooket.com

Discord: Originally a platform for online gamers, Discord is a voice and text communication app. Conversations can be organized into themes or specific questions. Students need to download the app and join the course once the instructor creates the Discord space. Available for iOS and Android.

Flip (Formerly Flipgrid): A free video discussion app from Microsoft. Small groups can share videos for learning and community building. info.flip.com

Flippity: A free, online, game-building tool. Create Jeopardy, MadLibs, Bingo, Flash Cards, Word Searches, and more. Flippity.net

Jamboard: Google-based digital whiteboard. Students can insert images, text, shapes, and digital sticky notes. A great collaborative brainstorming tool. Available via GoogleSuite.

Kahoot: The free, go-to multiple-choice game for online and f2f classes. Images can be added to each question and music can be customized. Leaderboards are created at the conclusion of each question. Kahoot.it

Kritik: A paid platform that integrates with the major LMS providers. Instructors post assignments, and after students submit, they are assigned peers' assignments to review and provide feedback in a timely manner. All submissions and feedback among students is anonymous. Kritik boasts the development of students' critical thinking skills and self-reflection via peer review. Kritik.io

Mentimeter: Interactive presentation software for quizzes, polls, word clouds, and more. https://www.mentimeter.com/

Nearpod: A presentation tool that facilitates slide-based teaching either in class or remotely. It can integrate with GoogleSlides, Microsoft PowerPoint, and YouTube. Slides that include quizzes or checkpoints can be added to the slide deck. The basic package is free, but upgrades are available.

Padlet: A free, online notice board that can contain links, videos, images, and documents. Great for organization, brainstorming, making mood boards, keeping notes, or blogging. Padlet.com

Perusall: A social e-reading tool that makes coursework more socially interactive (read: fun and engaging). The platform promises that students will be more intrinsically motivated to do assignments with classmates before class. Sharon's students report that "it's actually kind of fun," which is high praise. Perusall.com

Socrative: A free web platform in which instructors can present quizzes, polls, questions, study questions, and formative assessments. The instructor can see results in real-time and both individual and group results. Pryke's (2020) students found that Socrative helped with studying and student-to-student interaction.

Icebreakers for Face-to-Face and Online Environments

The following playful activities are discipline non-specific and may be used in a variety of contexts.

Speed dating: Create two circles of students: an inner circle and an outer circle. Each student on the inside should be facing a student on the outside. Present a question to the whole group and ask each pair to discuss their responses. Set a timer for 3–5 minutes and then ask students on the outside circle to move one over so that they are opposite a different partner. You could present a new question or the same one and repeat the process. Either way, students have the opportunity to get a variety of perspectives from their colleagues.

Midnight Snack: Give students access to a Google Jamboard and ask them to post their favorite midnight snack. When everyone is done, organize them by theme (chocolate, chips, sweet, salty, etc) to determine the favorite snack vibes in the group.

Introduce Your Pet: Designate the first five minutes of an online class to pet introductions. Sharon has done this with her students and has met the expected dogs and cats, but also birds, ferrets, fish, and even a boyfriend.

Quick polls: In online classes, the polling feature in Zoom is easy and results are shared quickly. Start with a controversial question: Is cereal soup? Are hot dogs a sandwich? Spotify or Apple Music? Instagram or TikTok? The chat will blow up, guaranteed.

Quips and Canned Jokes

Did you hear that scientists figured out how to weigh a rainbow? *Turns out it's pretty light.*

When he first started performing, Neil Diamond went by the name "Neil Coal." . . . but then the pressure got to him.

I dropped my toothpaste this morning. I was Crestfallen.

What do you call a duck that does drugs? A *quackhead.*

What sound does a cow make when it runs out of milk? *None. There is udder silence.*

What kind of doctor is Dr. Pepper? A *fizzician.*

What do you call the offspring of an elephant and a rhino? *'Ell if I know.*

Earth is 70 percent water and most of it is uncarbonated, so technically, the Earth is flat.

What's the difference between black-eyed peas and chickpeas? *Black Eyed Peas can sing us a song, but chickpeas can only hummus one.*

Sundays are always a bit sad. But the day before is a sadder day.

Did you hear about the cheese factory that blew up in France? All that was left was de Brie.

Why don't French people eat two eggs for breakfast? *Because one egg is un oeuf.*

What is the leading cause of dry skin? *Towels.*

Did you know you can use disposable masks to make espresso? *Turns out they're coughy filters.*

How do you cut a pizza without a pizza cutter? *You use Little Caesars.*

I accidentally drank a bottle of invisible ink and spent the weekend sitting in the ER waiting to be seen.

I'm getting my significant other a fridge for their birthday. I can't wait to see their face light up when they open it.

Every night after work, a doctor goes to the same bar and orders a chestnut daiquiri. One night, the bar is out of chestnuts, so the bartender uses hickory instead. The doctor is disgusted and says "What is this?!?" The bartender replies "It's a hickory daiquiri, doc."

Where did Noah keep the bees? *In the ark-hives.*

You've heard of Murphy's Law, but have you heard of Cole's Law? It's pretty much just cabbage and mayonnaise.

What do Winnie the Pooh and Alexander the Great have in common? *Same middle name.*

My significant other and I brush our teeth together every morning, because 9 of 10 dentists say that brushing your teeth alone will not prevent cavities.

What starts with an E, ends with an E, but only has one letter in it? *Envelope.*

I just got a new book of puns about Africa. You're Ghana love them!

Why are vampires so easy to fool? *Because they're suckers!*

Notes

Introduction

1. He did not cite his sources in APA format. He didn't even cite in MLA, Chicago, Turabian, IEEE, or any combination of any random referencing style. But we're giving it a pass.

2. At least one of this book's authors is secure enough to know that he is no longer completely aware of what is hip. He has only recently, and begrudgingly, stopped making references to the TV show *Cheers* in class. (It is entirely feasible that this show was on the air when the *parents* of current post-secondary students were born. It is not a timely reference.)

3. Except for classes like ours, obviously, which are fun.

4. And, if we're lucky, teaching.

5. Yes, that's his official name.

6. Playing cribbage is practically a requirement of retirement.

7. One of this book's authors argues that all college and university courses should make students more interesting at parties and is a legitimate motivator. She's even had students report back after graduation saying that they discussed course concepts at a party/dinner/date (all of which went well, were not boring, and two of which resulted in marriages!).

8. The alliteration of the three P's also makes it easy to remember and fun to say.

9. But the book does include an Appendix of jokes and activities that have worked for others.

10. Of course, we'll cite our sources: We're not charlatans.

11. Keith really wanted to write, "This model does not imply that instructors must become the next Don Rickles," but he was voted down. Sharon doesn't even know

who that is, so Keith is clearly showing his age. Readers should email Sharon to tell her that the Don Rickles line is way funnier.

12. Like Don Rickles.

Chapter 1

1. It has been used to educate adults, too. The computer game Minesweeper was included on PCs for twenty years in order to train computer users to use a mouse.
2. Each of these elements connects to the legs of the stool—play, playfulness, and positivity. It's like it was planned!
3. "Never make predictions, especially about the future."—Yogi Berra
4. A practice heartily endorsed for this book.
5. And certainly, everyone does NOT love pineapple on pizza. Don't even start a conversation in class about this. It will end in fisticuffs. It's been tried.
6. Honestly!
7. If you want to skip ahead to those chapters, feel free. We're not cops.
8. This is essentially a mic-drop statement.
9. Yes, it's a real study! Yang, Pham, Choo, & Hu (2014). Duration of urination does not change with body size. Proceedings of the National Academy of Sciences, 111(33): 11932–11937.
10. In some cases, it's still all about chalkboards, but let's be optimistic.
11. Plans F through Z may also be warranted.
12. This story may or may not have happened to one of the authors.
13. Gender-neutral pronouns are used here to protect the individual's anonymity (but it wasn't Sharon).
14. The authors are on a mission to eliminate classrooms with bolted seats and stationary desks, but so far the campaign has been fruitless.
15. If you want to be all technical about it, this is Expectancy Theory. In a nutshell, the idea is that we tend to engage in behaviors we expect will lead to outcomes we value. Here, the focus is specifically on fun.
16. This is, again, why Sharon fought Keith about the Don Rickles reference. She'd rather refer to Pete Davidson, but Keith would probably have to Google the current cast of SNL.
17. Don't bother denying it. We all do it.
18. "Kids these days" definitely know AC/DC, despite their heyday being in the 1980s.
19. Yes, Rich was a headbanger in the 1980s. He grew up and cut his hair, so no one from high school would even recognize him now.
20. Trying to do so is an un-fun prospect if there ever was one.
21. It's like the whole premise of the book. Just keep reading, though, as we'll continue to make the case.

Chapter 2

1. See what we did there? See chapter 4 on Playfulness for more on laughter and humor.
2. In Canada, this is called "shinny." Sharon wanted to use that word here just to see if anyone looked it up, but Keith wanted to be inclusive of all readers, regardless of ice skating and slapshot ability.
3. Remember the old saying "Growing old is mandatory; growing up is optional."
4. Hmm . . . Perhaps next year's writing project has just presented itself.
5. Sharon's dad makes the best apple pie ever. It's a northern Italian recipe from his nonna. Keith respectfully disagrees and nominates his mother's apple pie.
6. To be honest, at least one of the authors might break into hives if a definition is not provided for such a key term as "play."
7. This is an incredibly well-crafted simile that is also super-meta if you are at all familiar with that masterpiece of modern cinema called *Forrest Gump*.
8. Of course, this isn't entirely true. Everyone does loads of things that are neither fun nor work, but such hyperbole will get this book quoted in the popular press.
9. Though, ideally, learning should be directly driven by intrinsic motivators, but there you have it . . .
10. Sharon's eldest refuses to play Uno, SkipBo, or Catan with her because Sharon doesn't "play to win." This might also be why Keith is terrible at Fortnite unless he has a really ruthless partner. Cue Sharon's youngest.
11. How? ". . . through dopamine dysregulation, particularly in the presence of serotonergic deficiency" (Koeners & Francis, 2020, p. 145). We're not sure what this means, but it sounds important and science-y.
12. There's, like, a whole chapter on fun in this very book!
13. Google it if you don't believe us. We are not the Seinfeld Wikipedia.
14. Since you are already reading the book, you could always check out the chapter on Playfulness for tips!
15. A discussion of active learning would require more pages than we have been allowed. Briefly, active learning is a bigger category than play, but one in which play exists. In other words, you're being honest if you call your play activities "active learning."

Chapter 3

1. When students were asked to choose their top fear, they selected death most often.
2. Keith played a lot of Fortnite during the writing of this book. For research only, obviously.
3. Sharon does not play Fortnite. For her, this analogy of trying again is exemplified in cooking, when she will try something new, tweak it, add this or that spice or

seasoning, and then make notes about how to improve it next time. Her children do not complain when she does this with cookies, brownies, cakes, or pies.

4. There are also playfulness scales for children (Lieberman, 1977; Barnett, 1990), adolescents (Staempfli, 2005) and older adults (Yarnal & Qian, 2011), but we made the executive decision to decide that in the post-secondary context, "adults" is the best term to use.

5. Sharon really wanted to add a clause here indicating that extroverts like her might be more playful. However, Keith is the world's most introverted introvert, and he's playful, so that got cut. The world is not binary. Nonetheless, the Big 5 Personality Traits are connected to playfulness in complex ways. That's another book idea on the list.

6. We are equating "adult" with "serious" here, and we realize that this is by no means a given. Both Sharon and Keith are both chronological adults and are also decidedly un-serious. In other words, we evoke the wise quip that "Growing old is mandatory, but growing up is optional," which is attributed to either Walt Disney, Chili Davis, or an anonymous internet personality.

7. How ironic!

8. Gamification was discussed in the chapter "Play." Just in case you are some sort of non-sequential reader.

9. Pun intended.

10. Pun also intended.

11. This is also the dictionary definition, but the Ludic Pedagogy definition sounds cooler.

12. "Humor can be dissected as a frog can, but the thing dies in the process and the innards are discouraging to any but the pure scientific mind."—E. B. White

13. Sharon wanted to include a reference to Olivia Newton-John here, but Keith thought that this was too suggestive for academics.

14. Just be glad that Keith doesn't have your cell phone number. He texts Sharon Dad jokes most days, because his wife taps out after about three in succession (which is usually by about 10 a.m. CST). When Sharon taps out, he sends them to her kids. They humor him with gifs and emojis.

15. This one is probably true. It wasn't in Bakar and we haven't identified any other secondary sources, but we bet it's true. Studies forthcoming.

16. Sharon loves double negatives and despite being a grammar aficionado, argues that sometimes the double negative makes things a lot clearer. Or perhaps better said, not using a double negative makes things not as able to be understood.

17. No matter how much you love the joke. Telling it again probably won't help. Trust me.

18. Hey! This sounds suspiciously like "playfulness"!

19. And doing so is just good advice regardless of who you are, what job you have, and whether you like pineapple on your pizza or not.

20. See? Chicken and egg.

21. Sharon and her students call their self-designed project a "thing," because that could mean anything, but that's probably not the best term, either. At least it's not a negative. Naming suggestions welcomed!

22. And split infinitives, apparently.

23. "Purportedly" because we found the quote on the internet, and no one really knows if stuff on the internet is true.

Chapter 4

1. We acknowledge that for some, including Sharon's mom, apples, oranges, and bananas are more likely to result in a good mood, and there's even research indicating that a diet rich in fatty fish, fruits, legumes, and vegetables can help to alleviate depression. But we like the ice-cream metaphor because it is more fun than any salmon metaphor could possibly be.

2. Like, a LOT of it. Really. Just try and read it all. Or even a fraction of it. There is a lot.

3. And final for this book. The literature goes on and on. The point has been made, but it'll be made here again: Student motivation and affect are inextricably bound.

4. We're looking at you, Linear Algebra.

5. Really, it was a phone booth. But "glass case of emotion" is indicative of his state of mind.

6. Really. We have heard this runaway train of thought more times than we can count. Every semester someone is convinced that it will happen to them.

7. We are going all-out with this example. Obviously.

8. Because Sharon thinks salt is "spicy."

9. See chapter "Implementation and Impacts" for how to turn this garbage into gold.

10. See chapter "Implementation and Impacts" again. We put lots of good stuff there.

11. Most of us can probably think of examples from our own experience. Who hasn't had a class they disliked because the prof was a miserable #$&*#@?

12. Infect in a GOOD way.

13. See examples at Sharon's website: www.sharonlauricella.com. This is how we are getting around any image permission issues.

14. Keith included. He is, by no measure, an accountant. Asking him to even think about the topic can bring him to tears.

Chapter 5

1. A quick search for #construction #dance on TikTok shall reveal amusing results. Try it.

2. And those are just published reports. We can all remember episodes from our university days that are indicative of students' mental health needs, regardless of how long it has been since our formal education. If you didn't experience something yourself, you probably knew someone who did.

3. Which we endorse completely but require a full staff to take on this project. Applications are open.

4. These are only examples, of course. A brief survey of the available tools suggests there are about 13 quintillion available, more or less.

5. LEGO is his preferred building block, but one works with the tools available.

6. Bonus feature of this activity: the look on students' faces when they walk into class to and see a beer pong table set up.

7. That's wild! Read it again. Even just *thinking* about playfulness has benefits! Think about a time you had fun and it positively affects your well-being. I'm doing it right now and I'm absolutely giddy.

8. Keith does not have a fitness watch. He leaves this focus on technology to Sharon and her need to beat all three rings on her Apple Watch every day.

9. And unwelcome!

10. Also a helpful solution for the most introverted students in the class.

11. But it also does not NOT propose it.

12. The model doesn't explicitly disapprove of them either.

13. For a complete conversation with Chris Whittaker, check out the Ludic Pedagogy podcast—The Ludicast!

14. There are other more unpleasant symptoms which we have chosen not to include here. You know what they are.

Chapter 6

1. Not really, but it sounds good.

2. However, the ability to bust out factoids about Amazonian tree frogs will liven up any dinner party.

3. If you're not down with our hip slang, that means "throw it away."

4. This assumption may be a stretch in some cases.

5. Assuming you don't decide to scrap the assignment altogether.

6. You're forgiven if you haven't designed them to be fun—you're still only reading this book!

7. Heck, it probably will!

8. Maybe this paragraph should have come with a content warning. Apologies.

9. Systemic change is a big, hairy beast that needs to be discussed a lot, by a lot of people in a lot of places. But this book is not one of those places.

Conclusion

1. "Quiet Quitting," a different but seemingly related issue, only compounds this issue. We'd like to dig into both of these topics further, but there is only so much room in *this* book. Wink, wink.

2. This was always going to be the end point of that metaphor, whether we liked it or not.

3. If we want a new metaphor, we could say "Never skip leg day when implementing Ludic Pedagogy."

4. To whom the issues of privilege also apply: not every faculty member will have the same level of privilege to explore a ludic practice.

References

Al Fatta, H., Maksom, Z., & Zakaria, M. H. (2019). Game-based learning and gamification: Searching for definitions. *International Journal of Simulation: Systems, Science & Technology, 19*. https://doi.org/10.5013/ijssst.a.19.06.

Almon, J. (2004). The vital role of play in early childhood education. In S. Howard (Ed.), *The developing child: The first seven years* (pp. 85-94). Waldorf Early Childhood Association of North America.

Altbach, P. G., Reisberg, L., & Rumbley, L. E. (2009). *Trends in global higher education: Tracking an academic revolution – A report prepared for the UNESCO 2009 World Conference on Higher Education.* UNESCO.

American College Health Association (2016). *American College Health Association-National College Health Assessment II: Canadian Reference Group Data Report Spring 2016.* American College Health Association.

Arnett, J. J. (2000). Emerging adulthood: A theory of development from the late teens through the twenties. *American Psychologist, 55*(5), 469-480. https://doi.org/10.1037/0003-066x.55.5.469

Aronson, J., Fried, C. B., & Good, C. (2002). Reducing the effects of stereotype threat on African American college students by shaping theories of intelligence. *Journal of Experimental Social Psychology, 38*(2), 113-125. https://doi.org/10.1006/jesp.2001.1491

Aschbacher, K., O'Donovan, A., Wolkowitz, O. M., Dhabhar, F. S., Su, Y., & Epel, E. (2013). Good stress, bad stress and oxidative stress: Insights from anticipatory cortisol reactivity. *Psychoneuroendocrinology, 38*(9), 1698-1708. https://doi.org/10.1016/j.psyneuen.2013.02.004

Ashby F. G., Isen, A. M., & Turken, A. U. (1999). A neuropsychological theory of positive affect and its influence on cognition. *Psychological Review, 106*(3), 529-550. https://doi.org/10.1037/0033-295x.106.3.529

Aylor, B. & Opplinger, P. (2003). Out-of-class communication and student perceptions of instructor humor orientation and socio-communicative style. *Communication Education*, 52(2), 122-134. https://doi.org/10.1080/03634520302469

Bakar, F. (2019). Appropriate and relevant humour in the university classroom: Insights from teachers and students. *European Journal of Humour Research*, 7(4), 137-152. https://doi:2010.7592/EJHR2019.7.4.bakar

Banas, J. A., Dunbar, N., Rodriguez, D., & Liu, S. (2011). A review of humor in educational settings: Four decades of research. *Communication Education*, 60(1), 115-144. https://doi.org/10.1080/03634523.2010.496867

Barnett, L. A. (1990). Playfulness: Definition, design, and measurement. *Play & Culture*, 3, 319-336.

Barnett, L. A. (2007). The nature of playfulness in young adults. *Personality and Individual Differences*, 43(4), 949-958. https://doi.org/10.1016/j.paid.2007.02.018

Barnett, L. A. (2012). Playful people: Fun is in the mind of the beholder. *Imagination, Cognition and Personality*, 31(3), 169-197. https://doi.org/10.2190/ic.31.3.c

Barret, T. (2005). Who said learning couldn't be enjoyable, playful and fun. In E. Poikela & S. Poikela (Eds.), *PBL in Context–Bridging Work and Education* (pp. 159-176). Tampere University Press.

Bateman, C. (Ed.). (2009). *Beyond game design: Nine steps toward creating better videogames*. Cengage Learning.

Bateson, P. (2014). Play, playfulness, creativity and innovation. *Animal Behavior and Cognition*, 1(2), 99-112. https://doi.org/10.12966/abc.05.02.2014

Bateson, P. & Nettle, D. (2014). Playfulness, ideas, and creativity: A survey. *Creativity Research Journal*, 26(2), 219-222. https://doi.org/10.1080/10400419.2014.901091

Bean, J. P. (2005). Nine themes of college student retention. In Seidman, A. (Ed.), *College student retention: Formula for student success* (pp. 215-243). ACE & Praeger.

Beaudette, T. (2016, September 9). Nearly 70% of university students battle loneliness during school year, survey says. *Canadian Broadcasting Corporation*. http://www.cbc.ca/news/canada/manitoba/university-loneliness-back-to-school-1.3753653?cmp=rss

Benjelloun, H. (2009). An empirical investigation of the use of humor in university classrooms. *Education, Business and Society: Contemporary Middle Eastern Issues*, 2(4), 312-322. https://doi.org/10.1108/17537980911001134

Blanco, C., Okuda, M., Wright, C., Hasin, D. S., Grant, B. F., Liu, S., & Olfson, M. (2008). Mental health of college students and their non-college-attending peers. *Archives of General Psychiatry*, 65(12), 1429-1437. https://doi.org/10.1001/archpsyc.65.12.1429

Bolkan, S., Griffin, D .J., & Goodboy, A. K. (2018). Humor in the classroom: The effects of integrated humor on student learning. *Communication Education*, 67(2), 144-164. https://doi.org/10.1080/03634523.2017.1413199

Bonnechere, B., Klass, M. Langley, C., & Sahakian, B. J. (2021). Brain training using cognitive apps can improve cognitive performance and processing speed in older adults. *Scientific Reports, 11*(1). https://doi.org/10.1038/s41598-021-91867-z

Brearley, F. Q. & Cullen, W. R. (2012). Providing students with formative audio feedback. *Bioscience Education, 20*(1), 22-36. https://doi.org/10.11120/beej.2012.20000022

Bronner, S. J. (2012). *Campus traditions: Folklore from the old-time college to the modern mega-university*. University Press of Mississippi.

Brown, S. (2010). *Play: How it shapes the brain, opens the imagination, and invigorates the soul*. Scribe Publications.

Browning, M.H. E. M., Larson, L. R., Sharaievska, I., Rigolon, A., McAnirlin, O., Mullenbach, L., Cloutier, S., Vu, T. M., Thomsen, J., Reigner, N., Metcalf, E. C., D'Antonio, A., Helbich, M., Bratman, G. N., & Alvarez, H. O. (2021). Psychological impacts from COVID-19 among university students: Risk factors across seven states in the United States. *PLOS ONE, 16*(1), e0245327. https://doi.org/10.1371/journal.pone.0245327

Buff, A., Reusser, K., Rakoczy, K., & Pauli, C. (2011). Activating positive affective experiences in the classroom: "Nice to have" or something more? *Learning and Instruction, 21*(3), 452-466. https://doi.org/10.1016/j.learninstruc.2010.07.008

Callaghan, P. (2004). Exercise: A neglected intervention in mental health care? *Journal of Psychiatric Mental Health Nursing, 11*(4), 476-483. https://doi.org/10.1111/j.1365-2850.2004.00751.x

Chabeli, M. (2008). Humor: A pedagogical tool to promote learning. *Curationis, 31*(3), 51-59. https://doi.org/10.4102/curationis.v31i3.1039

Chan, K. (2014, November 25). Beer(less) Pong Study Session: Rules and Guidelines. *KeithCChan.com*. https://www.keithcchan.com/2014/11/beerless-pong-study-session-rules-and-guidelines.html

Chandler, P. & Sweller, J. (1991). Cognitive load theory and the format of instruction. *Cognition and Instruction, 8*(4), 293-332. https://doi.org/10.1207/s1532690xci0804_2

Chang, C. (2013). Relationships between playfulness and creativity among students gifted in mathematics and science. *Creative Education, 4*(2), 101-109. http://dx.doi.org/10.4236/ce.2013.42015

Chiose, S. (2016, September 8). Reports of mental health issues rising among postsecondary students: study. *The Globe and Mail*. http://www.theglobeandmail.com/news/national/reports-of-mental-health-issues-rising-among-postsecondary-students-study/article31782301/

Christy, K. R., & Fox, J. (2014). Leaderboards in a virtual classroom: A test of stereotype threat and social comparison explanations for women's math performance. *Computers & Education, 78*, 66–77. https://doi.org/10.1016/j.compedu.2014.05.005

Clanton Harpine, E. (2015). Is intrinsic motivation better than extrinsic motivation? In E. Clanton Harpine, *Group-Centered Prevention in Mental Health: Theory, Training, and Practice* (pp. 87-107). Springer. https://doi.org/10.1007/978-3-319-19102-7_6

Clark, E. S. (2016, August 1). Herein lies a description of one of my favourite assignments: The unessay. *Emily Suzanne Clark: Researching & Teaching American Religions.* https://emilysuzanneclark.wordpress.com/2016/08/01/the-unessay/

Clark, R. (1972). *Einstein: The life and times.* Avon Books.

Clore, G. L., & Huntsinger, J. R. (2007). How emotions inform judgment and regulate thought. *Trends in Cognitive Science, 11*(9), 393-399. https://doi.org/10.1016/j.tics.2007.08.005

Condry, J. (1977). Enemies of exploration: Self-initiated versus other-initiated learning. *Journal of Personality and Social Psychology, 35*(7), 459-477. https://doi.org/10.1037/0022-3514.35.7.459

Cornillie, F., Jacques, I., De Wannemacker, S., Paulussen, H., & Desmet, P. (2011). Vocabulary treatment in adventure and role-playing games: A playground for adaptation and adaptivity. In S. De Wannemacker, G. Clarebout, & P. De Causmaecker (Eds.), *Interdisciplinary approaches to adaptive learning: A look at the neighbours. ITEC 2010. Communications in Computer and Information Science* (Vol. 126). Springer. https://doi.org/10.1007/978-3-642-20074-8_11

Cowan, B., Sabri, H., Kapralos, B., Porte, M., Backstein, D., Cristancho, S., & Dubrowski, A. (2010). A serious game for total knee arthroplasty procedure, education and training. *Journal of CyberTherapy & Rehabilitation, 3*(3), 285-298.

Craig, S. D., Graesser, A. C., Sullins, J., & Gholson, B. (2004). Affect and learning: An exploratory look into the role of affect in learning with AutoTutor. *Journal of Educational Media, 29*(3), 241-250. https://doi.org/10.1080/1358165042000283101

Csikszentmihalyi, M. (1975). Play and intrinsic rewards. *Journal of Humanistic Psychology, 15*(3), 41-63. https://doi.org/10.1177/002216787501500306

Datu, J. A. D. (2017). Peace of mind, academic motivation, and academic achievement in Filipino high school students. *The Spanish Journal of Psychology, 20*(e22), 1-8. https://doi.org/10.1017/sjp.2017.19

Deci, E., Koestner, R., & Ryan, R. (1999). A meta-analytic review of experiments examining the effects of extrinsic rewards on intrinsic motivation. *Psychological Bulletin, 125*(6), 627-668. https://doi.org/10.1037/0033-2909.125.6.627

Denial, C. (2019). The unessay. *Cate Denial.* https://catherinedenial.org/blog/uncategorized/the-unessay/

DeWolfe, C. E. J., Scott, D. & Seaman, K. A. (2020). Embrace the challenge: Acknowledge a challenge following negative self-talk improves performance. *Journal of Applied Sport Psychology, 33*(5), 527-540. https://doi.org/10.1080/10413200.2020.1795951

Dichev, C. & Dicheva, D. (2017). Gamifying education: What is known, what is believed and what remains uncertain: A critical review. *International Journal of Educational Technology in Higher Education, 14*(9). https://doi.org/10.1186/s41239-017-0042-5

Dobrogosz, H. (2012, July 25). 27 public speaking horror stories that are giving me major secondhand embarrassment. *Buzzfeed.* https://www.buzzfeed.com/hannahdobro/public-speaking-horror-stories

Dubey, R., Mehta, H., & Lombrozo, T. (2021). Curiosity is contagious: A social influence intervention to induce curiosity. *Cognitive Science, 45*(2), 1-16. https://doi.org/10.1111/cogs.12937

Dwyer, K. K. & Davidson, M. M. (2012). Is public speaking really more feared than death? *Communication Research Reports, 29*(2), 99-107. https://doi.org/10.1080/08824096.2012.667772

Eaton, L. G. & Funder, D. C. (2003). The creation and consequences of the social world: An interactional analysis of extraversion. *European Journal of Personality, 17*(5), 375-395. https://doi.org/10.1002/per.477

Eberle, S. G. (2014). The elements of play: Toward a philosophy and a definition of play. *Journal of Play, 6*(2), 214-233.

Feldman, J. (2019). *Grading for equity: What it is, why it matters, and how it can transform schools and classrooms*. Corwin.

Ferchmin, P. A. & Eterovic, V. A. (1982). Play stimulated by environmental complexity alters the brain and improves learning abilities in rodents, primates and possibly humans. *Behavioral and Brain Sciences, 5*, 164-165. https://doi.org/10.1017/s0140525x00011031

Fincham, B. (2016). *The sociology of fun*. Palgrave Macmillan.

Fine, G. A. & Corte, U. (2017). Group pleasures: Collaborative commitments, shared narrative, and the sociology of fun. *Sociological Theory, 35*(1), 64-86. https://doi.org/10.1177/0735275117692836

Fisher, K., Hirsh-Pasek, K., Golinkoff, R. M., Singer, D., & Berk, L. E. (2011). Playing around in school: Implications for learning and educational policy. In A. Pellegrini (Ed.), *The Oxford handbook of play* (pp. 341-363). Oxford University Press.

Forbes, L. K. (2021). The process of play in learning in higher education: A phenomenological study. *Journal of Teaching and Learning, 15*(1), 57-73. https://.doi.org/10.22329/jtl.v15i1.6515

Forbes, L. K. & Thomas, D. (Eds.). (2022). *The PlayBook: Professors at play*. ETC Press. https://press.etc.cmu.edu/books/professors-play-playbook

Francis, M. (2013). Using fun to teach rigorous content. *Communications in Information Technology, 6*(2), 151-159. https://doi:10.15760/comminfolit.2013.6.2.125

Frein, S. T., Jones, S. L., & Gerow, J. E. (2013). When it comes to Facebook there may be more to bad memory than just multitasking. *Computers in Human Behavior, 29*(6), 2179–2182. https://doi.org/10.1016/j.chb.2013.04.031

Friere, P. & Ramos, M. B. (1970). *Pedagogy of the oppressed*. Continuum.

Georganta, K. & Montgomery, A. (2016). Exploring fun as a job resource: The enhancing and protecting role of a key modern workplace factor. *International Journal of Applied Positive Psychology, 1*(1), 107-131. https://doi.org/10.1007/s41042-016-0002-7

Gibbons, M. M. & Woodside, M. (2012). Addressing the needs of first-generation college students: Lessons learned from adults from low-education families. *Journal of College Counseling, 17*(1), 21-36. https://doi.org/10.1002/j.2161-1882.2014.00045.x

Glynn, M. A. & Webster, J. (1992). The adult playfulness scale: An initial assessment. *Psychological Reports*, 71(1), 83-103. https://doi.org/10.2466/pr0.71.5.83-103

Gordon, G. (2014). Well played: The origins and future of playfulness. *American Journal of Play*, 6(2), 234-266.

Guitard, P., Ferland, F., & Dutil, E. (2005). Toward a better understanding of playfulness in adults. *OTJR: Occupation, Participation and Health*, 25(1), 9-22. https://doi.org/10.1177/153944920502500103

Hammer, D. (1997). Discovery learning and discovery teaching. *Cognition and Instruction*, 15(4), 485-529. https://doi.org/10.1207/s1532690xci1504_2

Hernandez, E. (2022, March 6). Colorado universities strain to keep up with students' ever-increasing demand for mental health resources. *Denver Post*. https://www.denverpost.com/2022/03/06/counseling-mental-health-resources-colorado-university/

Holmes, E. A., O'Connor, R. C., Perry, V. H., Tracey, I., Wessely, S., Arseneault, L., Ballard, C., Christensen, H., Silver, R.C., Everall, I., Ford, T., John, A., Kabir, T., King, K., Madan, I., Michie, S., Przybylski, A. K., Shafran, R., Sweeney, A., Worthman, C. M., Yardley, L., Cowan, K., Cope, C., Hotopf, M., & Bullmore, E. (2020). Multidisciplinary research priorities for the COVID-19 pandemic: A call for action for mental health science. *Lancet Psychiatry*, 7(6), 547-560. https://doi.org/10.1016/S2215-0366(20)30168-1

hooks, b. (1994). *Teaching to transgress: Education as the practice of freedom*. Routledge.

Hu, D. L., Lefton, L., & Ludovice, P. J. (2017). Humor applied to STEM education. *Systems Research and Behavioral Science*, 34(3), 216-226. https://doi.org/10.1002/sres.2406

Huberman, A. (2022, February 7). Using play to rewire and improve your brain (No. 58) [Audio podcast episode]. In *Huberman Lab Podcast*. https://youtu.be/BwyZIWeBpRw

Hung, S., Tsai, J. C., & Chou, S. (2016). Decomposing perceived playfulness: A contextual examination of two social networking sites. *Information & Management*, 53(6), 698-716. https://doi.org/10.1016/j.im.2016.02.005

Inyat, A. & Ali, A. Z. (2020). Influence of teaching style on students' engagement, curiosity and exploration in the classroom. *Journal of Education and Educational Development*, 7(1), 87-102. http://dx.doi.org/10.22555/joeed.v7i1.2736

Isen, A. M., Daubman, K. A., & Nowicki, G. P. (1987). Positive affect facilitates creative problem solving. *Journal of Personality and Social Psychology*, 52(6), 1122-1131. https://doi.org/10.1037/0022-3514.52.6.1122

Iwasaki, Y. (2006). Counteracting stress through leisure coping: a prospective health study. *Psychology, Health & Medicine*, 11(2), 209-220. https://doi.org/10.1080/13548500500155941

Jhangiani, R. & DeRosa, R. (n.d.). Open pedagogy examples. *Open Pedagogy Notebook*. https://openpedagogy.org/examples/

Johns, M., Schmader, T., & Martens, A. (2005). Knowing is half the battle: Teaching stereotype threat as a means of improving women's math performance. *Psychological Science*, 16(3), 175-179. https://doi.org/10.1111/j.0956-7976.2005.00799.x

Jones, C. [@ccjones13] (2017, April 18). *1. I've spent last few days grading student "unessays" for the US history survey (to 1877) + want to highlight a few of my favorites.* [Thread] [Tweet]. Twitter. https://twitter.com/ccjones13/status/854449018272751618

Jung, W. H., Kim, S. N., Lee, T. Y., Jang, J. H. Choi, C., Kang, D., & Kwon, J. S. (2013). Exploring the brains of Baduk (Go) experts: Gray matter morphometry, resting-state functional connectivity, and graph theoretical analysis. *Frontiers in Human Neuroscience*, 7. https://doi.org/10.3389/fnhum.2013.00633

Kay, R., Banks, L., & Craig, C. (2021). Examining the role of emotions in learning with technology. *14th annual International Conference of Education, Research and Innovation (ICERI2021)* (pp. 1817-1822). IATED Digital Library. https://doi.org/10.21125/iceri.2021.0486

Kessler, R. C., Berglund, P., Demler, O., Jin, R., Merikangas, K. R., & Walters, E. E. (2005). Lifetime prevalence and age-of-onset distributions of DSM-IV disorders in the National Comorbidity Survey Replication. *Archives of General Psychiatry*, 62(6), 593-602. https://doi.org/10.1001/archpsyc.62.6.593

Koeners, M. P. & Francis, J. (2020). The physiology of play: Potential relevance for higher education. *International Journal of Play*, 9(1), 143-159. https://doi.org/10.1080/21594937.2020.1720128

Kolb, A.Y. & Kolb, D.A. (2010). Learning to play, playing to learn: A case study of a ludic learning space. *Journal of Organizational Change Management*, 23(1), 26-50. https://doi.org/10.1108/09534811011017199

Kraepelien, M., Mattsson, S., Hedman-Lagerlöf, E., Petersson, I., Forsell, Y., Lindefors, N., & Kaldo, V. (2018). Cost-effectiveness of internet-based cognitive–behavioural therapy and physical exercise for depression. *BJPsych Open*, 4(4), 265-273. https://doi.org/10.1192/bjo.2018.38

Laamarti, F., Eid, M., & El Saddik, A. (2014). An overview of serious games. *International Journal of Computer Games Technology*, 2014, Article 358152. https://doi.org/10.1155/2014/358152

Laipply, J. (2019). About Judson. *Judson Laipply CSP*. https://www.judsonlaipply.com/

Lawson, A. P., Mayer, R. E., Adamo-Villani, N., Benes, B., Lei, X., & Cheng, J. (2021). The positivity principle: Do positive instructors improve learning from video lectures? *Educational Technology Research and Development*, 69(6), 3101-3129. https://doi.org/10.1007/s11423-021-10057-w

Lauricella, S. (2022). Equitable assessment in online environments. In R. Kay & B. Hunter (Eds.), *Thriving online: A guide for busy educators*. Ontario Tech University. https://doi.org/10.51357/CEFD2689

Lauricella, S., & Edmunds, T. K. (2022a). Ludic Pedagogy: Taking a serious look at fun in the COVID-19 classroom and beyond. *Educational Considerations*, 48(1). https://doi.org/10.4148/0146-9282.2324

Lauricella, S., & Edmunds, T. K. (2022b). Ludic Pedagogy online: Fun, play, playfulness, and positivity. In R. Kay & B. Hunter (Eds.), *Thriving online: A guide for busy educators*. Ontario Tech University. https://doi.org/10.51357/hgjk8068

Lauricella, S. & Kay, R. H. (2022). Fair and formative feedback in online learning. In R. Kay & B. Hunter (Eds.), *Thriving online: A guide for busy educators*. Ontario Tech University. https://doi.org/10.51357/dlsc5521

Leather, M., Harper, N., & Obee, P. (2021). A pedagogy of play: Reasons to be playful in postsecondary education. *Journal of Experiential Education, 44*(3), 208-226. https://doi.org/10.1177/1053825920959684

Lewis, B. A., Schuver, K., Dunsiger, S., Samson, L., Frayeh, A. L., Terrell, C. A., Ciccolo, J. T., & Avery, M. D. (2018). Rationale, design, and baseline data for the Healthy Mom II Trial: A randomized trial examining the efficacy of exercise and wellness interventions for the prevention of postpartum depression. *Contemporary Clinical Trials, 70*, 15-23. https://doi.org/10.1016/j.cct.2018.05.002

Lieberman, J. N. (1977). *Playfulness: Its relationship to imagination and creativity*. Academic Press.

Linnenbrink, E. A. (2007). The role of affect in student learning: A multi-dimensional approach to considering the interaction of affect, motivation, and engagement. In P. A. Schutz & R. Pekrun (Eds.), *Emotions in Education* (pp. 107-124). Academic Press. https://doi.org/10.1016/b978-012372545-5/50008-3

Lucardie, D. (2014). The impact of fun and enjoyment on adult's learning. *Procedia – Social and Behavioral Sciences, 142*, 439-446. https://doi.org/10.1016/j.sbspro.2014.07.696

Lunau, K. (2012, September 5). Mental health crisis on campus: Canadian students feel hopeless, depressed, even suicidal. *Macleans*. https://www.macleans.ca/education/uniandcollege/the-mental-health-crisis-on-campus/

Madgett, P. J. & Belanger, C. H. (2008). First university experience and student retention factors. *Canadian Journal of Higher Education, 38*(3), 77-96. https://doi.org/10.47678/cjhe.v38i3.503

Mani, A., Mullainathan, S., Shafir, E., & Zhao, J. (2013). Poverty impedes cognitive function. *Science, 341*(6149), 976-980. https://doi.org/10.1126/science.1238041

McGonigal, J. (2010). *Reality is broken: Why games make us better and how they can change the world*. Jonathan Cape.

McManus, I. C. & Furnham, A. (2010). "Fun, fun, fun": Types of fun, attitudes to fun, and their relation to personality and biographical factors. *Psychology, 1*(3), 159-168. https://doi.org/10.4236/psych.2010.13021

Middleton, J. A., Littlefield, J., & Lehrer, R. (1992). Gifted students' conceptions of academic fun: An examination of a critical construct for gifted children. *Gifted Child Quarterly, 36*(1), 38-44. https://doi.org/10.1177/001698629203600109

Mikkelsen, K., Stojanovska, L., Polenakovic, M., Bosevski, M., & Apostolopoulos, V. (2017). Exercise and mental health. *Maturitas, 106*, 48-56. https://doi.org/10.1016/j.maturitas.2017.09.003

Moschella, M. & Radnofsky, C. (2020, April 16). Locked-down citizens around the world dress up to take out the trash in online meme. *NBC News.* https://www.nbcnews.com/news/world/locked-down-citizens-across-world-dress-take-out-trash-online-n1185011

Nickerson, C., Diener, E., & Schwarz, N. (2010). Positive affect and college success. *Journal of Happiness Studies, 12*(4), 717-746. https://doi.org/10.1007/s10902-010-9224-8

Nouchi, R., Taki, Y., Takeuchi, H., Hashizume, H. Nozawa, T., Kambara, T., Sekiguchi, A., Miyauchi, C. M., Kotozaki, Y., Nouchi, H., & Kawashima, R. (2013). Brain training game boots executive functions, working memory and processing speed in young adults: A randomized controlled trial, *PLosOne, 8*(2). https://doi.org/10.1371/journal.pone.0055518

O'Donnell, D. P. (2018, September 28). The unessay. *Daniel Paul O'Donnell: Teaching.* https://people.uleth.ca/~daniel.odonnell/Teaching/the-unessay

Oliver, E. J., Markland, D., & Hardy, J. (2010). Interpretation of self-talk and post-lecture affective states of higher education students: A self-determination theory perspective. *British Journal of Educational Psychology, 80*(2), 307-323. https://doi.org/10.1348/000709909x477215

Ortiz Berry, M. (2022, January 19). The day I came to class dressed as Athena: The pedagogy of fun. *Wabash Center.* https://www.wabashcenter.wabash.edu/2022/01/that-day-i-came-to-class-dressed-as-athena-the-pedagogy-of-fun/

Pale, P. (2013). Intrinsic deficiencies of lectures as a teaching method. *Collegium Antropologicum, 37*(2), 551-559.

Papert, S. (1996). *The connected family: Bridging the digital generation gap.* Longstreet Press.

Pekrun, R. (2006). The control-value theory of achievement emotions: Assumptions, corollaries, and implication for educational research and practice. *Educational Psychology Review, 18*(4), 315-341. https://doi.org/10.1007/s10648-006-9029-9

Pekrun, R. (2011). Emotions as drivers of learning and cognitive development. In R. A. Calvo & S. K. D'Mello (Eds.), *New perspectives on affect and learning technologies* (pp. 23-39). Springer. https://doi.org/10.1007/978-1-4419-9625-1_3

Petelczyc, C. A., Capezio, A., Wang, L., Restubog, S. L. D., & Aquino, K. (2017). Play at work: An integrative review and agenda for future research. *Journal of Management, 44*(1), 161-190. https://doi.org/10.1177/0149206317731519

Pfeffer, A. (2016, September 26). Ontario campus counsellors say they're drowning in mental health needs. *Canadian Broadcasting Corporation.* https://www.cbc.ca/news/canada/ottawa/mental-health-ontario-campus-crisis-1.3771682

Philippot, A., Dubois, V., Lambrechts, K., Grogna, D., Robert, A., Jonckheer, U., Chakib, W., Beine, A., Bleyenheuft, Y., & De Volder, A. G. (2022). Impact of physical exercise on depression and anxiety in adolescent inpatients: A randomized controlled trial. *Journal of Affective Disorders, 301*, 145-153. https://doi.org/10.1016/j.jad.2022.01.011

Pichlmair, M. (2008). Venturing into the borderlands of playfulness. *Technoetic Arts, 6*(2), 207-212. https://doi.org/10.1386/tear.6.2.207_1

Plass, J. L., Homer, B. D., & Kinzer, C. K. (2015). Foundations of game-based learning. *Educational Psychologist, 50*(4), 258-283. https://doi.org/10.1080/00461520.2015.1122533

Plester, B., Cooper-Thomas, H., & Winquit, J. (2015). The fun paradox. *Employee Relations, 37*(3), 380-398. https://doi.org/10.1108/er-04-2013-0037

Podilchak, W. (1991). Distinctions of fun, enjoyment and leisure. *Leisure Studies, 10*(2), 133-148. https://doi.org/10.1080/02614369100390131

Pratt, I., Harwood, H., Cavazos, J., & Ditzfeld, C. (2019). Should I stay or should I go? Retention in first-generation college students. *Journal of College Student Retention: Research, Theory & Practice, 21*(1), 105-118. https://doi.org/10.1177/1521025117690868

Pressman S. D., Matthews, K. A., Cohen, S., Martire, L. M., Scheier, M., Baum, A., & Schulz, R. (2009). Association of enjoyable leisure activities with psychological and physical well-being. *Psychosomatic Medicine, 71*(7), 725-732. https://doi.org/10.1097/psy.0b013e3181ad7978

Provine, R. R. (2000). *Laughter: A scientific investigation*. Penguin Books.

Proyer, R. T., Brauer, K., Gander, F., & Chick, G. (2021). Can playfulness be stimulated? A randomized placebo-controlled online playfulness intervention study on effects on trait playfulness, well-being, and depression. *Applied Psychology: Health and Well-Being, 13*(1), 129-191. https://doi.org/10.1111/aphw.12220

Pryke, S. (2020). The use of Socrative in university social science teaching. *Learning and Teaching, 13*(1), 67-86. https://doi.org/10.3167/latiss.2020.130105

Purinton, E. F. & Burke, M. M. (2019). Student engagement and fun: Evidence from the field. *Business Education Innovation Journal, 11*(2), 133-140.

Ratey, J. (2008). *Spark: The revolutionary new science of exercise and the brain*. Little, Brown.

Reynolds, L. (2022). 20 ways to provide effective feedback for learning. *Teachthought*. https://www.teachthought.com/pedagogy/20-ways-to-provide-effective-feedback-for-learning/

Ruch, W. (1998). Foreword and overview. The sense of humor: A new look at an old concept. In W. Ruch (Ed.), *The sense of humor: Explorations of a personality characteristic* (pp. 3-14). De Gruyter Mouton. https://doi.org/10.1515/9783110804607-003

Schaefer, C. & Greenberg, R. (1997). Measurement of playfulness: A neglected therapist variable. *International Journal of Play Therapy, 6*(2), 21–31. https://doi.org/10.1037/h0089406

Seligman, M. E. & Adler, A. (2018). Positive education. In S. Paculor (Ed.), *Global happiness policy report 2018* (pp. 53-74). Sustainable Development Solutions Network.

Shankland, R. & Rosset, E. (2017). Review of brief school-based positive psychological interventions: A taster for teachers and educators. *Educational Psychology Review, 29*(2), 363-392. https://doi.org/10.1007/s10648-016-9357-3

Sharpe, L. L. (2005). Play does not enhance social cohesion in a cooperative mammal. *Animal Behaviour, 70*, 551-558. https://doi.org/10.1016/j.anbehav.2004.08.025

Sharpe, L. L. & Cherry, M. I. (2003). Social play does not reduce aggression in wild meerkats. *Animal Behaviour, 66*, 989-997. https://doi.org/10.1006/anbe.2003.2275

Shaw, C. A. & McEachern, J. C. (Eds.). (2000). *Toward a theory of neuroplasticity*. Psychology Press.

Shen, X .S., Chick, G., & Zinn, H. (2014). Playfulness in adulthood as a personality trait. *Journal of Leisure Research, 46*(1), 58-83. https://doi.org/10.1080/00222216.2014.11950313

Sheu, F. & Grissett, J. (2022). Increasing motivation for learning through non-disposable assignment: A student perspective. In T. Bastiaens (Ed.), *EdMedia + Innovate Learning Proceedings*. Association for the Advancement of Computing in Education (AACE). https://www.learntechlib.org/noaccess/221394/

Siviy, S. M. & Panskepp, J. (2011). In search of the neurobiolgoical substrates for social playfulness in mammalian brains. *Neuroscience and Biobehavioral Reviews, 35*(9), 1821-1830. https://doi.org/10.1016/j.neubiorev.2011.03.006

Spariosu, M. (1989). *Dionysus reborn: Play and the aesthetic dimension in modern philosophical and scientific discourse*. Cornell University Press.

Staempfli, M. B. (2005). Adolescent playfulness, leisure and well-being. *Dissertation Abstract International-A, 66* (06). (Publication No. AAT NR02952).

Starbuck, W. H. & Webster, J. (1991). When is play productive? *Accounting, Management and Information Technologies, 1*(1), 71-90. https://doi.org/10.1016/0959-8022(91)90013-5

Steele, C. M. & Aronson, J. (1995). Stereotype threat and the intellectual test performance of African Americans. *Journal of Personality and Social Psychology, 69*(5), 797-811. https://doi.org/10.1037/0022-3514.69.5.797

Stein, N. & Levine, L. (1991). Making sense out of emotion. In W. Kessen, A. Ortony & F. Kraik (Eds.), *Memories, thoughts, and emotions: Essays in honor of George Mandler* (pp. 295-322). Lawrence Erlbaum Associates, Inc.

Steinem, G. (2019). *The truth will set you free, but first it will piss you off! Thoughts on life, love, and rebellion*. Penguin Random House.

Stiglbauer, B., Gnambs, T., Gamsjäger, M., & Batinic, B. (2013). The upward spiral of adolescents' positive school experiences and happiness: Investigating reciprocal effects over time. *Journal of School Psychology, 51*(2), 231–242. https://doi.org/10.1016/j.jsp.2012.12.002

Sull, D., Sull, C., & Zweig, B. (2022, January 11). Toxic culture is driving the Great Resignation. *MIT Sloan Management Review*. https://sloanreview.mit.edu/article/toxic-culture-is-driving-the-great-resignation/

Sutton-Smith, B. (1997). *The ambiguity of play*. Harvard University Press.

Svinicki, M. D. (2004). *Learning and motivation in the postsecondary classroom*. Anker Publishing Company.

Sweller, J. (1988). Cognitive load during problem solving: Effects on learning. *Cognitive Science, 12*(2), 257-285. https://doi.org/10.1207/s15516709cog1202_4

Talbert, R. (2015). Specifications grading: We may have a winner. *Robert Talbert, Ph.D.* https://rtalbert.org/specs-grading-iteration-winner/

Tews, M. J., Jackson, K., Ramsay, C., & Michel, J.W. (2015). Fun in the college classroom: Examining its nature and relationship with student engagement. *College Teaching, 63*(1), 16-26. https://doi.org/10.1080/87567555.2014.972318

Tews, M. J., Michel, J. W., & Noe, R. A. (2017). Does fun promote learning? The relationship between fun in the workplace and informal learning. *Journal of Vocational Behavior, 98*, 46-55. https://doi.org/10.1016/j.jvb.2016.09.006

Thompson, S. (2022). Digital toolbox for online learning. In R. Kay & B. Hunter (Eds.), *Thriving online: A guide for busy educators*. Ontario Tech University. https://doi.org/10.51357/IZIF9566

Um, E., Plass, J. L., Hayward, E. O., & Homer, B. D. (2011). Emotional design in multimedia learning. *Journal of Educational Psychology, 104*(2), 485-498. https://doi.org/10.1037/a0026609

Unilever. (2021). Ice Cream. https://www.unilever.com/brands/ice-cream/

Valentin, L. S. S. (2017). Can digital games be a way of improving the neuroplasticity in stroke damage? Can the adult brain grow new cells or rewire itself in response to a new experience? *Open Journal of Medical Psychology, 6*(2), 153-165. https://doi.org/10.4236/ojmp.2017.62013

Van Vleet, M. & Feeney, B. C. (2015). Play behavior and playfulness in adulthood. *Social and Personality Psychology Compass, 9*(11), 630-643. https://doi.org/10.1111/spc3.12205

Van Winkle, C. M. (2017). The effects of entertainment and fun on the visitor's free-choice learning experience. *Journal of Leisure Research, 46*(5), 644-651. https://doi.org/10.1080/00222216.2014.11950347

Wall, K. (2020). COVID-19 pandemic: Impacts on the work placements of postsecondary students in Canada. *StatCan COVID-19: Data to Insights for a Better Canada, Catalogue No. 45280001*. Statistics Canada.

Walsh, A. (2015). Playful information literacy: Play and information literacy in higher education. *Nordic Journal of Information Literacy in Higher Education, 7*(1), 80-94. https://doi.org/10.15845/noril.v7i1.223

Wanzer, M. B., Frymier, A. B., & Irwin, J. (2010). An explanation of the relationship between instructor humor and student learning: Instructional humor processing theory. *Communication Education, 59*(1), 1-18. https://doi.org/10.1080/03634520903367238

Waters, L. (2021). Positive education pedagogy: Shifting teacher mindsets, practice, and language to make wellbeing visible in classrooms. In M. L. Kern & M. L. Wehmeyer (Eds.), *The Palgrave handbook of positive education* (pp. 137-164). Palgrave Macmillan. https://doi.org/10.1007/978-3-030-64537-3_6

Watson, D. (2002). Positive affectivity. In C. R. Snyder & S. J. Lopez (Eds.), *Handbook of positive psychology* (pp. 106-119). Oxford University Press.

West, S. (2015). *Playing at work: Organizational play as a facilitator of creativity*. [Doctoral dissertation, Lund University]. https://lup.lub.lu.se/search/ws/files/5719680/8082561.pdf

Whitton, N. (2018). Playful learning: Tools, techniques, and tactics. *Research in Learning Technology, 26*. https://doi.org/10.25304/rlt.v26.2035

Whitton, N. & Langan, M. (2019). Fun and games in higher education: An analysis of UK student perspectives. *Teaching in Higher Education, 24*(8), 1000-1013. https://doi.org/10.1080/13562517.2018.1541885

Wiley, D. (2013, October 21). What is open pedagogy? *Improving Learning*. https://opencontent.org/blog/archives/2975

Wu, C., Jing, B., Gong, X., Mou, Y., & Li, J. (2021). Student's learning strategies and academic emotions: Their influence on learning satisfaction during the COVID-19 pandemic. *Frontiers in Psychology, 12*. https://doi.org/10.3389/fpsyg.2021.717683

Yang, P.J., Pham, J., Choo, J., & Hu, D.L. (2014). Duration of urination does not change with body size. *Proceedings of the National Academy of Sciences, 111*(33), 11932-11937. https://doi.org/10.1073/pnas.1402289111

Yarnal, C. & Qian, X. (2011). Older-adult playfulness: An innovative construct and measurement for healthy aging research. *American Journal of Play, 4*(1), 52–79.

Yim, J. (2016). Therapeutic benefits of laughter in mental health: A theoretical review. *The Tohoku Journal of Experimental Medicine, 239*(3), 243-249. https://doi.org/10.1620/tjem.239.243

Zhang, F. & Kaufman, D. (2015). The impacts of social interactions in MMORPGs on older adults' social capital. *Computers in Human Behavior, 51*, 495-503. https://doi.org/10.1016/j.chb.2015.05.034

Zheng, H., Li, J., Salmon, C. T., & Theng, Y. L. (2020). The effects of exergames on emotional well-being of older adults. *Computers in Human Behavior, 110*, 106383. https://doi.org/10.1016/j.chb.2020.106383

Zinn, W. (2008). Making fun of school, or why does learning have to be such a drag?: Six key elements for motivating learning. *International Journal of Learning: Annual Review, 15*(8), 153-160. https://doi.org/10.18848/1447-9494/cgp/v15i08/45911

Ziv, A. (1976). Facilitating effects of humor on creativity. *Journal of Educational Psychology, 68*(3), 318-322. https://doi.org/10.1037/0022-0663.68.3.318

Zyda, M. (2005). From visual simulation to virtual reality to games. *Computer, 38*(9), 25-32. https://doi.org/10.1109/mc.2005.297

Index

AC/DC, 18
active learning, 35, 111n15
affect, negative, 47, 60, 62, 63, 65–69; modeling, 70; positive aspects, 66
affect, positive. See positivity
Anchorman, 65
Animal House, 86
apple pie, 23
assessments: academic, xiv, 22, 33, 42, 50, 51, 68–69, 74, 90, 93–95; authentic, 96; disposability, 68, 92, 93. See also grades
Assiniboine Community College, 17, 62
attention, 45–46, 48–49, 62–63, 66, 81, 101
attitude, xv, 17, 38–41, 46, 48–49, 53, 60, 84, 86
authenticity, xvi, 48, 74, 102

beer pong, xii, 80–81
Brandon University, 70
Bushnell University, 16

California State University at Sacramento, 80
Calvinball, 27
Cambrian College, 6
The Chair, 60

challenge, 17, 22, 32, 38, 87, 103
childhood, xiii, 2, 21, 42, 84
Christopher Newport University, 83
Clark, Emily Suzanne, 51
cognitive/motivational model of affect, 62
cognitive load, 7, 8, 18, 48, 65–66, 72
cognitive load theory (CLT), 7–8
communication, 14, 33, 47–48, 63, 71
control, 26, 34, 68, 95
course content, 5–9, 18, 22, 34, 39, 42, 45, 47, 68, 70, 89–90
course context, 5–7, 18, 29, 34, 46, 48, 49, 55
course design, 31, 72, 86, 89, 90, 94, 97
COVID-19, 65, 76–77, 81, 86, 90, 98, 101
creativity, 17, 22, 28, 38, 44, 49–51, 63, 73, 103; divergent thinking, 48–50
curiosity, 33, 38, 44, 53–57, 60, 70; encouraging, 56, 70

Dawson College, 87
Demers, Justin, 62
Disney, Walt, 57
disposition, xv, 39–41
Doctor Strange in the Multiverse of Madness, 87
Dooley, 1

educational technology, 5, 17, 79, 84, 95
Einstein, Albert, 53, 90
Emory University, 1
emotions, xv, 7, 14, 30, 31, 59–62, 64–68, 74, 81, 87; academic, 64. See also positivity
empathy, 32, 63
engagement, xiii, 3, 6–7, 11, 17–19, 22, 35, 40, 46, 48, 60–61, 67, 84, 87, 95, 99
enjoyment, 1, 17–18, 22, 24, 30, 32, 40, 64, 68, 72, 75, 76, 78, 84, 86, 99
entertainment, xvi, 29, 41
equity, diversity, inclusion (EDI), 11, 15, 27, 43, 46, 47, 84, 98–100, 103
excitement, xiii, 2, 31, 60, 76

feedback, 68–69, 89, 94–95
freedom, 38–39, 49–51, 95, 103
fun, xii, xiv, 2, 9, 15, 18, 25, 27–28, 44, 67, 81, 86, 102, 104; activities, 5, 9, 15; benefits, 7, 19, 75; defining, 2–4; delivery, 5, 7; environments, 14; mandated, 4, 9; as a motivator, 3–4, 7, 12, 31; social aspects, 12–16; subjectivity, 3–4, 8, 15, 27. See also hard fun

games, xiii, 17, 21, 24, 29, 33, 78–79, 81, 84; board games, 79, 80; game-based learning, 29, 102; gamification, 29, 43; serious games, 29–30, 79
Good Will Hunting, 12
grades, 22, 29, 35, 42, 61, 63–64, 69, 76, 95
Great Resignation, 101, 104

hard fun, 17–18
humor, 3, 24, 27, 38–39, 41, 44–49, 102; appropriateness, 46–47; benefits, 46–49; definition, 44–45; relevance, 45–46; sense of, xvi, 38, 41
hybrid teaching, xiii, 6, 34

ice cream, 59, 73–74
imagination, 31, 50
Instructional Humor Processing Theory (IHPT), 45, 47

joy, xiii, 2, 21, 41, 60, 99

Kannen, Victoria, 55
killjoy, not being a, xiii, 2, 9, 22, 50, 65, 96

Laipply, Judson, xi
Langille, Aaron, 6
laughter, 17, 25, 46–49, 82
Laurentian University, 55
Lawrence Technological University, 24
learning, xiv, xv, 2, 6–8, 12, 17–18, 22, 26, 30–32, 42, 45–48, 62, 65, 99; comprehension, 18, 42, 46, 48; emotions, 62, 64–67; environment, xiii, xv, 5, 31–32, 44, 48–49, 55, 71, 102–3; outcomes, xv, 34–35; retention, xv, 18, 42, 45–46, 48; strategies, 62–63. See also assessments, academic
leisure, 75
Lincoln, Abraham, 12
Little, Rich, 17–18
ludic mindset, 103–4
ludic ontology, 104
Ludic Pedagogy: aims, 9, 17, 32, 84, 86–88, 99; definition, xiii; guiding principles, 89–96; implementation, 4, 89, 96–97, 103; model, xiii-xvi, 2, 30, 46–48, 53, 60, 102

Malvini Redden, Shawna, 80
Mann, Alison, 79
meaningfulness, 15–16, 94
memory, 7, 45, 62, 79
mental health, xii, 61, 76–78, 82–85, 87, 98–99
Meskill, Thomas, 81

modelling, 5, 9, 38, 41, 46–49, 57, 67, 70, 74, 93, 96–97, 103
models of education, xiv, 102
motivation, 2–3, 7, 12, 30, 47–48, 62, 64; extrinsic, xiv, 29, 31, 61, 101; intrinsic, xiv, 4, 22, 27–29, 31, 38, 40, 61, 67, 69, 101–2, 104

Netflix, 12, 60
neuroplasticity, 78, 82

O'Donnell, Daniel Paul, 50
online teaching, xiii, 5, 34–35, 76
Ontario Tech University, 13, 34, 78, 83
Orlowski, Edward, 24
Ortiz Berry, Melissa, 16

parties, xii, 86, 89–92
performance, academic, 14, 22, 33, 42, 61, 63–64, 69, 71–72, 79, 85
physical activity, 15, 32–33, 41, 82
play, xiii, xv, 21–22, 25, 30, 35, 38, 78–81; adults, 21, 41; benefits of, 7, 22, 30, 32–33, 35, 81; challenges, 33–34, 103; criteria, 25–27; defining, xv, 23–24; elements of, 24–25; incorporating into classroom, 31–33; voluntary nature of, 26, 28–30
playfulness, xv, 9, 30, 38, 44, 50, 53, 73, 81, 86, 103; benefits of, 40, 42, 46, 50, 55, 81; defining, xv, 38–41; elements of, 44; incorporating into classroom, 42, 73
Playfulness Scale for Adults, 38–39
pleasure, 12, 23, 24, 32, 38, 44, 75
positive pedagogy, 84–85
positivity, xv, 4, 14, 28, 30–31, 47, 59, 63, 67, 70, 79, 104; defining, xv, 59–60, 67; impacts, 61–63; rewarding, 73; self-talk, 70–72, 74; toxic, 60
privilege, 103
problem solving, 7, 17, 23, 32, 63
prosocial bonds, xii, 6, 35, 48, 80–82, 86, 99. See also sense of community

recipe: as metaphor, xvi, 19, 66, 96, 102
Redick, Kip, 83
rigor, xiii, 2, 17–18, 22, 50

safety, 10, 19, 22, 30–31, 46, 49, 84, 103
satisfaction, 6, 60, 66, 87
sense of community, 1, 14–15, 29–30, 86, 99
seriousness, 22, 42, 60
social interaction, xii, 4, 13–14, 16, 19, 55, 57, 80, 82, 85
social media, xi, 3, 11, 81, 90
spontaneity, 26, 33, 41, 43, 45
Steinem, Gloria, 34
stress, 1, 10–11, 28, 79, 86–87
student-instructor relationship, 46, 48
student retention, xii, 99, 101
student success, xvii, 16, 19, 68, 85
surprise, 31, 48, 56
syllabus, xiii, 72, 90

teaching philosophy, xvi
Twitter, 11, 61, 94–96

unessay, 50–51, 96
ungrading, 64, 69, 95
universal design, 99–100
University of Connecticut, 81
University of Lethbridge, 50
University of Maryland-College Park, 1
University of Toronto, 79
University of Waterloo, 40
University of Winnipeg, 94
urination, 8

video games, 17, 30, 79

wellness. See mental health
Whittaker, Chris, 86
Whose Line is it Anyways, 29
Williams, Robin, 12
Woodcock, Kathryn, 40

Author Bios

Dr. Sharon Lauricella is the inaugural Teaching Scholar in Residence at Ontario Tech University in Oshawa, Ontario, Canada. She holds a position as a Full Professor in the Faculty of Social Science and Humanities and is a scholar of Communication and Scholarship of Teaching and Learning. Sharon holds a doctoral degree from the University of Cambridge (UK) and a BA from Wheaton College (Massachusetts). A Canadian with Italian and American roots, Sharon will always cheer for the Red Sox and hopes that readers will not hold that against her.

Dr. Lauricella has been recognized for teaching excellence, having been awarded the Ontario Tech Teaching Award twice (2007 and 2012), the Faculty Teaching Award (2010 and 2019), and the Tim McTiernan Student Mentorship Award (2020). She loves being a faculty member not least because it is way easier than being in graduate school. That was hard.

Dr. T. Keith Edmunds was born early in life. With degrees in psychology, rural development, rural studies, and business, he has yet to determine a definite scholarly trajectory, which he is told is a good thing. After being awarded a PhD from the University of Guelph and an MBA from Laurentian University, both in Canada, he found himself as an assistant professor at Brandon University, also in Canada. All the things for Keith took and take place in Canada.

Currently, Keith teaches in the Department of Business Administration at the aforementioned Brandon University, where he tries—*really hard*—to implement the tenets of Ludic Pedagogy in all the courses he teaches.

Dr. Edmunds would rather have dental surgery than write biographies of himself.

www.ingramcontent.com/pod-product-compliance
Lightning Source LLC
Chambersburg PA
CBHW030657230426
43665CB00011B/1128